# SI-RENITY

How I Stay Calm
and Keep the Faith

# SI ROBERTSON

HOWARD BOOKS
An Imprint of Simon & Schuster, Inc.

NEW YORK   NASHVILLE   LONDON   TORONTO   SYDNEY   NEW DELHI

Howard Books
An Imprint of Simon & Schuster, Inc.
1230 Avenue of the Americas
New York, NY 10020

First Howard Books trade paperback edition May 2017

HOWARD and colophon are trademarks of Simon & Schuster, Inc.

For information about special discounts for bulk purchases,
please contact Simon & Schuster Special Sales at 1-866-506-1949
or business@simonandschuster.com.

The Simon & Schuster Speakers Bureau can bring authors
to your live event. For more information or to book an event,
contact the Simon & Schuster Speakers Bureau at 1-866-248-3049
or visit our website at www.simonspeakers.com.

All photographs courtesy of the author

Manufactured in the United States of America

10  9  8  7  6  5  4  3  2  1

The Library of Congress has cataloged the hardcover edition as follows:

Names: Robertson, Si, 1948–  author.
Title: Si-renity : how I achieve peace and comfort through faith, family, and fun /
    Si Robertson.
Other titles: Serenity
Description: First Howard Books hardcover edition. | New York : Howard
    Books, 2016.
Identifiers: LCCN 2016013091 | ISBN 9781501135439 (hardback) |
    ISBN 9781501135446 (ebook)
Subjects: LCSH: Robertson, Si, 1948- | Television personalities—United States—
    Biography. | BISAC: BIOGRAPHY & AUTOBIOGRAPHY / Rich & Famous.
Classification: LCC PN1992.4.R5355 A3 2016 | DDC 791.4502/8092 [B]—dc23
LC record available at https://lccn.loc.gov/2016013091

ISBN 978-1-5011-3543-9
ISBN 978-1-5011-3546-0 (pbk)
ISBN 978-1-5011-3544-6 (ebook)

# CONTENTS

# PROLOGUE

Somebody told me that *Duck Dynasty* had made me a celebrity, and I didn't know exactly what that meant. I was told it meant I was famous—like the Kardashians or Charlie Sheen. Hey, if being a celebrity means I have to act like them, I don't want any part of it, Jack!

Since *Duck Dynasty* launched in 2012, my life really hasn't changed much. Sure, things are better for my family and me financially. Thanks to the Good Lord, we won't have to worry about paying a bill ever again, and that beats having to wonder how I'm going to pay my mortgage or utility bills, which is how it was for much of my life.

Even though I might have a few more dollars in my bank account, I'm still the same guy. I like fishing and duck hunting, and I enjoy the beauty of what God created. I still attend church every Sunday morning to thank the Almighty for what He has done and what He will do, and I'm continuing to share the Good News with as many people as I can.

It's my faith in God that helps me stay on an even keel. Hey, Jack, I learned a long time ago that I can count on His promise to be the same yesterday, today, and forever

(Hebrews 13:8). He is the one who held our family together when I was a kid and money was scarce. He is the one who stood beside me through all the trauma I experienced in Vietnam. He was there when I had my heart attack. He was even there when all the hoopla started with *Duck Dynasty*. He had a plan all along, and I'm just on for the ride.

Not only is God the same yesterday, today, and forever— but being the same yesterday, today, and tomorrow is one of my own goals. Even though our lives are now on display for all to see, and even though we have more money in our pockets than we did before, I find peace in knowing who I am and Who I belong to—and that will never change.

And hey, I'm still madly in love with the woman I married in 1971—in fact, we renewed our wedding vows in May 2014. Even after all the *Duck Dynasty* "fame," what I enjoy most is being with my wife, Christine, and the rest of my family—my brothers and sisters and their children, and my own kids and grandkids. Family is what matters most to me, and being with the Robertson family is what I love more than anything else in the world.

Even when we were children, my brothers and sisters and I were exceptionally close. Everything was centered at the dinner table. We ate together every night and discussed what happened during the day. Even today, we share many meals together.

I'll never forget a conversation I had when I was stationed in Germany with the United States Army. One of the soldiers who worked with me had to fly home on emergency leave to attend his father's funeral. He came back about a week later, and I could tell he was struggling emotionally.

*Because of my service in the Army during the*
*Vietnam War, I've always had an interest*
*in helping veterans and active soldiers.*

"Hey, why don't you go back home?" I said to him. "You still need time to grieve. You need to be with your family."

"Why would I want to be at home?" he said. "Why would I want to be there, watching my brothers and sisters fight over what little money my dad made?"

That conversation saddened me then, and it saddens me today. A lot of people believed *Duck Dynasty* wouldn't last as long as it has. They thought money and fame would rip our family apart, like it does to so many other families who appear on reality TV shows. But hey, they don't know the Robertson family. *Duck Dynasty* started as a family affair—and it will end as a family affair. And at the center of it all is our faith in the Almighty.

One thing that *has* changed in my life is that I'm able to be more generous. The Good Lord has blessed my family and me mightily, and I'm so glad I now have the financial means to help others who are in need. You'll read about some of the children's charities and ministries I'm involved with in the chapters that follow. It warms my heart to help others, especially kids.

Even when I didn't have a lot of money, I tried to help anyone I could. That might have meant fixing a neighbor's roof, mowing an elderly woman's lawn, or taking food to a needy family. Although I didn't have much in terms of money and material possessions, I tried to assist others whenever possible. It's what the Bible says we're supposed to do. *"Do not neglect to do good and to share what you have, for such sacrifices are pleasing to God"* (Hebrews 13:16).

Our country has gotten away from helping each other, and I think America would be such a better place if we got back to taking care of each other. The love of God should compel us to help one another. How can we not share what God has entrusted to us?

I still have a hard time believing the plan God had in store for me. Honestly, I could have never imagined it being like this. In Ephesians 3:20, God tells us, *"Now to him who is able to do immeasurably more than all we ask or imagine, according to his power that is at work within us, to him be glory in the church*

*and in Christ Jesus throughout all generations, for ever and ever!
Amen."*

Hey, it's true. God has blessed me more than I could have
ever imagined. I can't believe the people I've met, the places
I've been, and the things I've been able to do. Watching what
the Almighty has done with my family and how He uses us
strengthens my faith in Him even more, because I know that
none of these good things would have happened without
God's hand.

The Robertson family has made it our life's work to share
the Good News. During the past few decades, we have baptized hundreds of people in the Ouachita River in front of
my brother Phil's house. It's the most important thing we do
as Christians. The fact that God put us on TV has enabled
us to share His message with millions of people around the
world. If that's not God's work, I don't know what is.

Hey, Silas Merritt Robertson is a reality TV star. Think
about that for a minute, Jack! I look in the mirror every
morning, and I know it took divine intervention to make me
an international star. I tell people that if they don't believe in
God, they need to look at the Robertson family. Look at what
He had to work with, and look at what He has accomplished!

There were many times in my life when I was in a bind,
either financially or physically, but came out okay. I'll never
forget a time right after Christine and I were married. We
were broke and desperately needed money to pay our rent
and utilities. We were about to be evicted from our home,
and I didn't know where I was going to get the money to pay
the bills. I was feeling anything but peaceful and serene.

I dropped to my knees and prayed to God for help. It was the only thing I knew to do. When I checked the mail the next day, there was a check for five hundred dollars. I had accidentally overpaid my truck loan, and my credit union mailed me a refund. Looking back at it now, I believe it was part of God's plan for me. He was testing my faith in Him.

Hey, there was another time when Phil and his wife, Kay, were in similar dire circumstances. Duck Commander was still in its infancy, and Phil wasn't selling enough duck calls to pay his bills. He was behind on his mortgage and didn't have money for groceries to feed his boys. "Well, I guess I better go to the bank and ask for a loan," Kay told him.

"Nah, wait until the mail comes," Phil told her. "I think there's going to be a check in there."

"Why would there be a check?" Kay asked him. "Nobody owes us any money." But they reached out to our Heavenly Father in prayer, and He heard them.

When the mail arrived, there was an eight-hundred-dollar check from somebody in Japan who was ordering one hundred duck calls. Their prayers for help were answered.

Sure, having financial security is nice, but money and fame haven't changed who I am. My faith is what brings me peace and si-renity.

*The peace of God, which transcends all understanding,*

*will guard your hearts and your minds in Christ Jesus.*

—Philippians 4:7 (NIV)

# CHAPTER 1

# SI-RENITY

In January 2005, I suffered a heart attack while duck hunting with my brother Phil and his sons. I knew something was very wrong with me, but I went home and climbed into bed. Hey, I'll admit it wasn't the smartest thing I've ever done. When I woke up the next morning, my chest pains were so severe that I told Christine to take me to the emergency room.

After doctors examined me and put a camera down my throat, they told me I needed open-heart surgery. My left main coronary artery was completely blocked. Doctors told me I had what they call a "widow-maker," which could kill me any minute.

It's a miracle I didn't die. I smoked cigarettes for more than thirty years, and the bad habit finally caught up with me. I had ignored the warning signs for a long time. I had been suffering heartburn for quite a while, and I was eating antacids like they were M&M's. Having heartburn didn't really make sense because I've always had an cast-iron stomach. Despite my wife's urging, I never went to the doctor to find out what was wrong.

So, there I was, lying in a hospital bed, not knowing if I was going to survive to see another sunrise. Surgeons were going to crack open my chest to save my life, and I was scared to death. I thought I might die right there in that hospital bed.

In fact, I was such a nervous wreck that my blood pressure was going through the roof. It was a Saturday, and the heart surgeon was hoping to wait until Monday to perform the procedure with his regular team of doctors.

"If you don't settle down," he told me, "I'll have to take you in there right now and do it on my own. I promise, you don't want that to happen."

After hearing his warning, I closed my eyes, took a deep breath, and tried to calm down.

*This is stupid,* I told myself. *Here I am worried about something I can't control. The Almighty has taken care of my family and me my entire life. He's certainly going to take care of me now when I need him most.*

Then I prayed to God: *Hey, let me first say thank you. Thank You for bringing me into this world. Thank You for my parents, my brothers and sisters, my wife, and my children. Thank You for my job and my friends. You have watched over me my entire life, and I know You're watching over me now. Hey, I'm just along for the ride, and it has been a good one.*

Thankfully, my heart settled down with the help of medication, and then I fell asleep. I slept most of the next day and woke up just as nurses were preparing to take me in for surgery.

The procedure lasted several hours. The surgeons took a vein from my leg and used it to bypass a blockage and get blood to my heart. Thankfully, the Almighty sent very skilled surgeons, doctors, and nurses to save my life. It was another one of God's miracles. Just as I'd prayed, the Lord watched over me and protected me.

After my surgery, I never picked up another cigarette. I promised my wife, children, and the rest of the Robertson clan that I would stop, and that's exactly what I did. Overall, I'm in pretty good health for my age. I think it's because of the work we do on Phil's land. It's great exercise and keeps me in good physical shape.

_After my surgery, I never picked up another cigarette._

When I remember my conversation with God on that hospital bed, I'm reminded of the "Serenity Prayer," which was written by Protestant theologian Reinhold Niebuhr in 1951. It has been adopted by Alcoholics Anonymous and is used to help a lot of addicts. I think it can help anyone who is searching for peace and tranquility.

*God grant me the serenity*
*to accept the things I cannot change;*
*courage to change the things I can;*

*and wisdom to know the difference.*
*Living one day at a time; enjoying one moment at a time;*
*Accepting hardships as the pathway to peace;*
*Taking, as He did, this sinful world*
*as it is, not as I would have it;*
*Trusting that He will make all things right*
*if I surrender to His Will;*
*That I may be reasonably happy in this life*
*and supremely happy with Him*
*Forever in the next.*
*Amen.*

Too many times, this sinful world tries to steal our joy with addictions, disease, suffering, and other problems. Hey, Jack, nobody is going to steal my joy. My joy comes from knowing that God is the Father and His Son is Jesus Christ. As it says in Romans 15:13: *"May the God of hope fill you with all joy and peace as you trust in him, so that you may overflow with hope by the power of the Holy Spirit."*

My faith is pretty simple: I believe Jesus Christ came to this earth and became flesh to save you and me from our sinful ways. Jesus left our Father's side, came to the world as flesh, and died on the cross to pay for what you and I have done wrong. We're weak and can't help ourselves, so Jesus paid the ultimate price for our sins.

Three days after Jesus Christ died on the cross, He rose from the dead and walked out of his tomb. He spent forty days and forty nights with five hundred people to prove His resurrection. Some people even watched His body ascend to heaven.

It was all part of God's plan. Jesus came to earth of His free will and knew what He had to do to save us. He paid for our sins and then ascended into the heavens. Right now, Jesus is sitting at our heavenly Father's side.

---

Jesus' story is my story too; and it's either true or false.

---

That's His story and it's my story too, and it's either true or false. For those of us who have researched it, we know that there's more evidence for its being true than for its being false. Hey, I can simply look at creation and the constellations to know it's true.

I can go out west to Montana, Wyoming, and South Dakota, far away from city lights and pollution, and see stars in the clear night sky. Some of them are millions of miles from Earth, but I can see that they're perfectly aligned to form a man who is pulling back a bow and arrow (Sagittarius) or a man who is pouring water from a jug (Aquarius). If you look closely enough, you can see a lion (Leo), hunter (Orion), bull (Taurus), and scorpion (Scorpius). Those are designs, and that means there is a designer. God created everything, and Jesus came to planet Earth.

My faith in Jesus Christ is based on facts and eyewitness

accounts, Jack! As I go through life, I share Jesus Christ's story of death, burial, and resurrection with as many people as I can. That is what Matthew 28:19 tells us to do as Christians: *"Therefore go and make disciples of all nations, baptizing them in the name of the Father and of the Son and of the Holy Spirit."*

No matter my troubles or circumstances, I know the Almighty can bring me serenity, courage, and wisdom. God can do it for you too, but we have to surrender ourselves to Him and allow Him to do it. It doesn't do us any good to get stressed out about situations we can't control.

---

No matter my troubles or circumstances, I know the Almighty can bring me serenity, courage, and wisdom.

---

Hey, if God was going to take me after my heart attack, it was going to happen, and there wasn't anything I could have done about it. Romans 8:28 taught me that God is in control of all things in my life. He is sovereign over all: *"We know that in all things God works for the good of those who love him."*

My faith in the Almighty brings me more peace and serenity than anything else in this life. As it says in 1 Peter 1:8, *"Though you have not seen him, you love him; and even though you do not see him now, you believe in him and are filled with an inexpressible and glorious joy."*

I've come to know that I can only control my own actions.

I can control what I think about and what my reactions will be to certain situations, but God controls everything else. Even though we might feel like life has thrown a truckload of heartache or trouble at us, we have to realize that we don't have control over what's happening around us and we don't have control over others' actions. We can't change other people; they have to change themselves.

Hey, relax and don't take things so seriously. Have fun and be joyful. People go through stress-filled lives trying to fill voids with sex, drugs, money, and careers. The only thing that can fill the voids in our lives is our faith in Jesus Christ.

---

Hey, relax and don't take things so
seriously. Have fun and be joyful.

---

My faith in the Almighty was never stronger than two years ago when I lost two of my brothers in the span of thirteen months. My brother Harold died of complications from Alzheimer's disease on October 27, 2013. He was seventy-four years old. Then my oldest brother, Jimmy Frank, died of a sudden heart attack on November 21, 2014, at the age of seventy-eight.

These brothers were two of my heroes. Both of them served in the United States Air Force and attended Louisiana State University. Jimmy Frank served in the air force out of high school, and then used the GI Bill to pay his way through

LSU. Harold went to LSU and then joined the air force after college.

Harold and Jimmy Frank proved to us younger kids that we were capable of escaping poverty and making better lives for ourselves. They were great role models. Hey, I give my parents, James and Merritt Robertson, a lot of credit for the way they raised us. Even though we were poor, they stressed the importance of education, especially my mother. I wish I had listened to her advice more closely over the years.

After Jimmy Frank and Harold graduated from LSU, my other older brothers, Tommy and Phil, enrolled at Louisiana Tech University in Ruston, Louisiana. They played on the football team together, and Phil graduated with a bachelor's degree in physical education and a master's degree in education. I enrolled at Louisiana Tech in 1967, but was more interested in having a good time while I was there. I dropped out of college after only three quarters, and then Uncle Sam sent me to Vietnam in October 1968.

Jimmy Frank earned a master's degree in journalism from LSU and became an accomplished writer. He wrote for newspapers in Louisiana and Texas for more than fifty years, as well as trade publications and corporate magazines. He also wrote a book about Phil's life—*The Legend of the Duck Commander: The Life and Times of Phil Robertson*. This book was revised to become *Happy, Happy, Happy* and was published in 2011. Jimmy Frank and his wife, Connie, lived in Elgin, Texas, and had six sons and eight grandchildren. Jimmy Frank was a caring man and loved being outdoors as much as we do.

Harold loved God, his family, the outdoors, and LSU football, probably in that order. He was an officer in the air force and had a successful professional career in many areas. Harold worked as a Boy Scout district executive, high school coach and administrator, plant manager, home health administrator, and politician. More than anything else, Harold loved people and had a gift for bringing them together and leading them. After Harold's retirement, he became a preacher and shared the Good News with many folks in Farmerville, Louisiana.

Harold spent the last few months of his life at the War Veterans Home in Monroe, Louisiana. It pained me to see the toll that Alzheimer's disease took on my big brother. Harold and his wife, Mary, were married for forty-six years and had two daughters and two grandchildren.

My siblings and I have always been very close. I put that at my mother's feet. Whenever I fought with one of my brothers or sisters when I was a kid, which wasn't very often, my momma liked to recite 1 John 4:20: *"Whoever claims to love God yet hates a brother or sister is a liar. For whoever does not love their brother and sister, whom they have seen, cannot love God, whom they have not seen."* I loved my older brothers very much.

Even though I miss seeing Harold and Jimmy Frank and spending time with them, I don't grieve their deaths. Both of my parents are gone, and my older sister Judy Gimber died of cancer in 2006. She was sixty-four. I mourned their deaths and was saddened when they left this earth, but I know in my heart that they trusted Jesus as their savior. Even though their bodies went into caskets and were buried in the ground, I know their spirits are with the Almighty.

I don't remember the specific days my parents, brothers, and sisters died. Because of my faith, their deaths were not catastrophic events for me. It might seem callous to hear someone say it, but not to me. Did their deaths affect me? Yeah, they affected me, but not like death might affect others. I know in my heart that they passed from this earth, and that I will see them again in heaven.

Hey, my faith in God provides me with steadfast belief that my life on this physical earth is only the beginning. I know I will have eternal life with the Almighty. I've told my wife and children, "When I die, don't go to my grave and mourn. My physical body might be there, but the essence of who I am will be with the Almighty."

The neatest thing about *Duck Dynasty* is that it has strengthened my belief in God. Through all the opportunities I've been given, I've seen Him do amazing things. For example, we've had dozens of kids come to us through the Make-A-Wish Foundation. Some of those kids were stricken with cancer, and we prayed with them for mercy and for God to heal their bodies. In some cases, the kids were cured of cancer.

People ask us all the time, "Why don't y'all get off the Gospel?" Hey, I've seen too much and experienced too much to not believe it and share it with others. I think Phil probably says it best: "All the money in the world will not get you out of the grave. All the fame in the world will not get you out of the grave. The only way to beat sin and death is by accepting Jesus Christ as your Lord and Savior."

Hey, Phil's right—that's the only way to beat the grave, Jack. It's my story, and I'm sticking to it.

# HALLU-SI-NATIONS
## Si-Language

Hey, if you're going to become part of my posse, you have to know two languages: English and Si-Language. The first one is easy enough to understand because it's America's native language. However, understanding Si-Language might be a little tricky for some. It's unique in itself and it's constantly evolving.

Of course, Si-Language is most famously known for its excessive use of "Hey," the most important word in my vocabulary. It's automatic. It's like a fabric woven into my character. "Hey" comes out when I open my mouth. It's a natural reflection.

Hey can mean yes, hey can mean maybe, hey can mean no, hey can mean next week. The bottom line is, you gotta understand me to understand hey. When you hear me say it, y'all give it the meaning you want it to have.

One of the most important aspects of understanding Si-Language is recognizing the emphasis of my words. Most of the time it's not about what I say, but how I say it and when I say it. Hey, I'll add the word "Jack" to the beginning, middle, or end of a lot of phrases. Depending on where I use it, Jack can mean a lot of things. I might say, "Best of luck with that, Jack" or "Hey, Jack, you can take that to the bank."

One of the first things you have to understand about my lingo is that when I greet people, I'll say, "What about it?" It basically means hello in passing, okay? It's my informal way saying, "What's up?" without really wanting to know the answer.

But if I'm talking to someone I have a prior relationship with, I might say, "All right, boys, what about it?" I'm basically asking my buddies what they've been doing lately. Have they killed any ducks or caught any fish? Have they watched any good TV crime dramas? When I open my greeting with "All right, boys," that means I want them to answer. I want them to be specific with their answers.

Now, if I say, "Okay, okay, okay," it means I might be nervous about something. It's pretty easy to recognize, and I'm not nervous very often. However, my use of *okay* gets a little complicated at times. I might say, "Okay, okay, okay," when I'm trying to prove my point. I use that approach quite often with my nephew Jase because his head is harder than concrete.

Another catchphrase I use a lot is "Yep, yep." When I use a double yep, it means I'm not really that interested in what someone is telling me. When I say, "Yep, yep," that means I'm ready for him or her to quit talking. If my sister-in-law Kay or nephew Alan is telling me a story that goes on forever, I'll say, "Yep, yep." That's the signal for them to quit talking. The faster the yeps come out, the faster I want them to shut their traps.

---

When I use a double yep, it means I'm not really that interested in what someone is telling me.

---

Now, I might be yepping at someone, but then I'll suddenly say, "Naw, naw." That means they've somehow piqued my interest in what they're telling me. When I say, "Hey, naw, naw," that means I want them to finish telling me their story because I'm entertained.

Hey, when I start sharing a story with someone, I'll usually start with, "No, no, hey." That's the cue for my boys to start listening because they're about to be mesmerized by what they hear! Hey, look here, I tell stories like an M. Night Come-along movie. My buddies know I'm usually setting them up for a big twist. When they hear, "No, no, hey," they realize they better start listening intently for details because the plot is about to get serious, Jack!

Of course, my wife, Christine, understands me better than anyone. When she's with me, she usually works as my translator. Plus, she might be the only person in the world who has figured out how to make me stop talking. When Christine is telling me something and I rudely interrupt her, she'll grab my hands and hold them down. Somehow, my mouth shuts. It's the only way to keep me quiet. Hey, it's easier said than done.

*You gave me life and showed me kindness,*

*and in your providence watched over my spirit.*

—JOB 10:12 (NIV)

# CHAPTER 2

# WORLD'S GREATEST FANS

Hey, what's the first thing a redneck does after he strikes it rich? He buys himself a new truck, guns, and a house, probably in that order. After *Duck Dynasty* became popular and my nephew Willie finally gave me a raise for being on the show, one of the first things I did was buy Christine a new home in West Monroe, Louisiana.

Now, you might be surprised to learn that it's not a very large house. Hey, I don't need one of those big, fancy estates like my nephews have. I live well outside the city limits in the country, and I'm only a few miles down the road from my brother Phil. There's a gas station down the street, and I can find about everything I need in there.

I bought us a new but modest manufactured home. There are a couple of bedrooms, a big living room, an open kitchen, dining room, and porches on the front and back of the house. It's everything Christine and I need—and more than we thought we'd ever have. There's no doubt the Good Lord has blessed us mightily.

Fortunately, one of the mobile home dealers in Monroe worked out a deal with me. I did some advertising and promotions for him, and he gave me a good deal on my new house. We put the new home on the same land where my old one once stood. While my old house was being bulldozed, the dealer put another mobile home on the lot next to me. Christine and I lived there until our new house was ready.

Hey, here's the only problem with living in a place like West Monroe: everyone in town knows exactly where I live. If *Duck Dynasty* fans visit West Monroe, they only have to go to a restaurant or gas station and ask somebody where I live. The local folks are kind enough to give them my exact address.

Hey, don't get me wrong. I don't mind everybody knowing where I live. It's nice to visit with fans that come by our house to see me, as long as they don't arrive after midnight! There have been more than a few occasions when fans knocked on my front door long after I was asleep. They'll knock loud enough to wake up Christine and me.

Well, one day Willie drove by my temporary home and noticed a lot of cars parked on the side of the road. He saw me posing for photographs in the front lawn with a big group of fans. When I went to work at Duck Commander the next day, Willie's secretary told me that he wanted me to build a fence around my house for security reasons.

"Hey, I already have a good security system," I told her.

"He still wants you to get a fence," she said. "Willie said he would pay for it."

Christine and I figured it might be time to get a privacy fence anyway. A few weeks earlier, she fell while working in the yard and broke her arm. One of our neighbors took photographs of her being carried away in an ambulance and sold them to the *National Enquirer*. Our neighbor even told the tabloid that I was standing in the front yard, crying. Hey, I was worried about my wife, but I wasn't weeping. I knew she was going to be fine.

Well, a couple of weeks after my conversation with Willie's secretary, there was a tall, white privacy fence all the way around my property. Hey, the contractor who built it must have thought I wanted to keep giraffes from looking into my windows. The fence is about ten feet tall! Willie about fell over when I handed him the bill; the fence cost more than thirty thousand dollars to build!

Hey, if I've learned anything during the past four years, it's that the vast majority of *Duck Dynasty* fans are the greatest fans in the world. Everywhere I go, it amazes me how genuinely nice and loyal our fans are. So many of our fans are just like us; they're hardworking and God-fearing Americans. They're the salt of the earth. I think that's a big reason there's such a connection between the Robertson family and the people who love watching our show.

I'll tell you something else: *Duck Dynasty* fans are some of the most generous people in the world. You wouldn't believe some of the items they have mailed to me. There was one *Duck Dynasty* episode in which Willie and I appeared on

Mountain Man's radio show. When we arrived at the station, there was a silver bell sitting on the counter. I rang it, and then I rang it again and again. Hey, I've always had a thing for bells. Some people have a foot fetish. Well, I have a bell fetish.

After that show aired on TV, I must have received five hundred bells in the mail from fans. There were Liberty Bells, cowbells, hand bells, sleigh bells, doorbells, and chocolate bells. I put them all around our house, and rang them every time I walked by one. Finally, Christine told me: "It's either me or the bells. They have to go." I thought to myself, *Man, I'm going to miss that woman.*

---

Finally, Christine told me: "It either me or the bells."
I thought to myself, *Man, I'm going to miss that woman.*

---

Perhaps the encounters with fans that tickle me most are when I meet people who recognize me, but don't know if I'm really Uncle Si from *Duck Dynasty*. It's like my name is on the tip of their tongues. Hey, I think I'm original. If there's a guy out there who looks like me, well, he's a lucky man, Jack!

Last fall, my friend Phillip McMillan and I were driving to go deer hunting in Texas, and we had my grandson Brady and his son Bryson with us. We stopped at a gas station in a small town so I could use the restroom. I was hungry, so I grabbed corn chips and a bag of ice for my tea. I put the stuff on the counter and reached into my pocket for money.

*One of my favorite charities is Homes of Hope for
Children in Purvis, Mississippi. I love what Dr. Michael
Garrett and his staff are doing for so many kids.*

"May I see your ID?" the lady behind the counter said.

"What do you need my ID for?" I asked.

"I just need to see your driver's license," she said.

"Hey, I'm not buying liquor," I said. "You don't need my ID."

"Sir, if you don't show me your driver's license, you can't
buy the ice or the corn chips," she said.

I didn't know what was going on, but I handed her my
driver's license. She looked at my ID, and then told the other
lady behind the counter, "You're right. It is Uncle Si!"

"What are you doing in this hick town?" she asked.

"Hey, I'm just trying to buy ice and corn chips," I said.

When Christine and I were visiting my son, Scott, and his family in Virginia one time, we took our four grandsons to a giant aquarium in Virginia Beach. Hey, it was one of the coolest places I've ever been. You could walk under the aquarium and look up and see sharks, tuna, stingrays, crabs, SpongeBob SquarePants, dolphins, and beluga whales. After a couple of hours of looking at the fish, it was dinnertime.

We walked into the cafeteria, and Scott told me to find a table in the corner. Well, a group of about five teenagers walked in. One of them did a double take when he saw me. I was wearing blue jeans, cowboy boots, and a cowboy hat.

I heard him tell his friends, "That's him! That's him!"

One of his buddies said, "No, it's not. What would he be doing in Virginia Beach?"

The kids walked up to me, and one of them said, "We know you."

"Yeah, you probably do," I said. "You've probably seen my TV show. It's called *Catch a Cow*."

"No, that's not it," one of the boys said. "What's the show about?"

"Look, that's the name of the show," I said. "I ride a horse on the show, and I'm trying to catch a longhorn in the brush. But I never catch it because he's so slick."

"Nah, the show has something to do with something that flies," said one of the boys. "It has something to do with ducks. Yeah, it's *Duck Dynasty*!"

"You got me," I said.

I spent a few minutes talking to the kids, and signed autographs and took a photo with them.

I spend a lot of days on the road appearing at speaking engagements and other events. It's a lot of work, but it's so much fun. Most of the people I meet are really nice, and they love our show, which makes me feel good. I try to meet as many fans as I can. If people are willing to wait in a line for four hours to get my autograph and shake my hand, then making sure they meet me is the least I can do. I love my fans, and *Duck Dynasty* certainly wouldn't be anything without them.

If people are willing to wait in a line for four hours to get my autograph and shake my hand, then making sure they meet me is the least I can do.

I'll never forget what happened during one of my appearances in South Carolina a couple of years ago. It was an outdoor event in the middle of the summer, and it was very hot and humid. Hey, it was so hot the bees were taking off their yellow jackets. After a couple of hours, people started fainting and falling out from heat exhaustion. It was so bad they had to call a few ambulances to take people to the hospital.

Well, there was a pregnant lady standing in line, and the medical people told her she had to leave. She was dehydrated, and the EMTs were worried about her and her baby. She refused to leave until she met me. So I climbed off the stage and went back to where she was sitting.

I smiled at the lady and said, "Hey, they tell me that you're not leaving until you see me."

"That's right," she told me. "You're my favorite person on *Duck Dynasty*."

"Well, I told them I'm not leaving until I get my picture taken with you," I told her.

The lady's eyes filled up with tears. She hugged me, and then I had a photograph taken with her. They took her to a hospital, and one of the organizers at the event later told me that she and her baby were doing fine.

I'm willing to do whatever it takes to make our fans happy. I'm a patient guy, and I think I have pretty good endurance for someone my age because I spend so much time working on Phil's land. We'll work on duck blinds, dams, and food plots for eight or ten hours a day in preparation for duck season. Hey, it takes a lot of work to shoot mallards out of the sky!

Of course, there have been a few *Duck Dynasty* fans that I'll never forget. In July 2013, I was asked to attend the Louisiana Outdoor Expo at the Cajundome in Lafayette, which is where the University of Louisiana–Lafayette Ragin' Cajuns play basketball. I sat at a booth and probably met more than three thousand people that day. I was supposed to sign autographs and pose for photographs for four hours, but I ended up staying two additional hours to take care of everybody.

When I was finally done with the event, I was exhausted. Hey, I'm not a young buck anymore. Phillip was with me, and he took me back to the greenroom to get ready to leave.

About the time I started falling asleep on a couch, I heard a knock at the door.

Phillip looked at one of the security guards in the room and told him, "Hey, we're done. No more pictures, and no more autographs. We were only supposed to stay for four hours and we've been here for six. Tell them no. I'll be the bad guy if I have to." Phillip wasn't being rude; he was only looking out for me. He knew my gas tank was empty.

The security guard opened the door and talked to the people outside. Then he said, "Phillip, you have to talk to these people. Please talk to them."

Phillip put on his game face and walked outside, closing the door behind him. There was a ten-year-old boy in the hallway, and his mom and dad told Phillip that he was dying of cancer. His parents said he was expected to live for just a few more months. They told Phillip that the only thing he wanted was to meet me. Phillip walked back into the green-room and told me, "Si, I know you're tired. But this is a big one." He told me about the boy.

"Bring him to me," I said.

The boy and his parents came into the room. He was wearing blue jeans, a green camouflage shirt, and a baseball hat. I took a couple of photographs with him and signed some autographs.

"Man, where have you been?" I asked him. "I've been waiting for you all day long!"

I ended up spending about thirty minutes with the boy before we left to fly back to Monroe. The boy's parents cried the entire time. I could tell they were tears of joy because they were so happy for their son. I could really feel the love in the room as I talked to him.

By the time we were ready to leave, there were probably fifteen to twenty people in the room. There were policemen, security guards, cleaning ladies, and event organizers. I stood up and told everyone, "Hey, come over here. This little man needs a powerful prayer, and we're going to appeal to the Almighty on his behalf."

———————————

"This little man needs a powerful prayer," I said, "and we're going to appeal to the Almighty on his behalf."

———————————

Everybody in the room came together and held hands, and I said a prayer for the boy. Phillip told me the prayer gave him goose bumps. I prayed: "Father, we are pleading with You on behalf of this boy to spare him. You control the molecular structure of his body, Father, and we know that all things are possible through You. Oh Lord, please show him favor and give him mercy. In Jesus' precious name we pray, amen."

I have to admit that my voice was cracking, and I was fighting back tears as I said the prayer that night. When I finished, there wasn't a dry eye in the room. Phillip told me later that it seemed like I was praying for my own child. Hey, as far as I'm concerned, every little girl and boy I meet is like my own. I love every one of them.

When we left the Cajundome that night, Phillip and I didn't talk about what happened. We both knew that the Almighty would either show the boy favor or guide him home to heaven. Either way, God had His arms around him and was going to take care of him.

About two years later, I flew to south Louisiana to appear at an event with Phillip, Jase, and Godwin. We flew to an airport and then took a helicopter to the event. When we arrived at the event, there was a crowd gathered to meet us. The first person to greet us was a handsome twelve-year-old boy with a big smile on his face.

"Hey, do you remember me?" the boy asked Phillip. "You prayed for me at the Cajundome."

"Si, do you know who this is?" Phillip asked me. "It's the boy from Lafayette."

Tears filled my eyes, and I walked over and hugged him. Miraculously, he had beaten cancer and was healthy again. Truthfully, I did not expect to see him again on this side of heaven. It was such a wonderful reunion, and I was so happy to see him. It was another reminder of God's love and strength.

Skye Loustalot was a beautiful thirteen-year-old girl when I met her. She was a big *Duck Dynasty* fan from Semmes, Alabama, and loved to watch our show while sitting in a recliner with a big bowl of popcorn. During the summer of 2013, she was diagnosed with osteosarcoma, a bone cancer. Doctors had to amputate her right leg, and she underwent surgery to remove a mass from her abdomen.

When we learned of Skye's illness, we made her a special video message, in which I told her how much we loved her and were praying for her. In November 2013, we met Skye at the Bay of Holy Spirit Jubilee in Fairhope, Alabama. She was very sick at the time, and the staff at University of South Alabama Children's and Women's Hospital arranged for her to come to the event via an ambulance.

When we met Skye, she was wearing a pink hoodie and was sitting up on a gurney. My nephew Alan, brother Phil, sister-in-law Kay, and my nephew Willie and his wife, Korie, were with me. Alan put his hands on Skye and prayed for her. He prayed, "I pray that You'll bless her with healing and restoration. I pray for her family tonight, Father. I pray that You'll lift them up in a very powerful way. We're so glad to meet her, Father, please give her courage in Jesus' name."

Tragically, Skye died in May 2014. She was fourteen years old. I'll never forget the courage she displayed that was so evident when we met her. More than anything, though, I'll always remember her sweet smile, laughter, and love for her parents and brothers. I pray that the moment we spent with her took her mind off her illness and brought joy to her heart. She was such a beautiful child in so many ways.

I know it's hard for some people to understand why there's so much suffering in the world. It's especially difficult to see children suffering through the pain from awful diseases like cancer. If I could take their suffering and pain away and trade places with them, I would do it in a second. Unfortunately, the only things we can do are put our arms around them and love them like Jesus.

While we might not understand why bad things happen, I know God created all things, raised Jesus from the grave, and controls everything. I know He will raise us from our graves on our last days on earth to be with Him forever. I put my trust in the Gospel of Jesus Christ and His death and resurrection. I know every one of us will eventually face death, but I trust in God and understand that He will ultimately heal us for eternity. I can't wait to see children like Skye in heaven.

# HALLU-SI-NATIONS
## Hot Tubs

I absolutely love meeting and spending time with *Duck Dynasty* fans, but it can be pretty exhausting work. At most of my events, I spend anywhere from four to six hours taking photographs and signing autographs. At the end of the day, my head hurts and my body aches.

I've tried several ways to unwind and relax on the road. I've tried yoga, stretching, running in place, meditation (that was kind of scary), taking a bath, and working out. It's probably the perfect time for a glass of wine or a cocktail to calm me down, but I quit drinking alcohol after I returned home from Vietnam. I haven't had a drink in more than thirty years.

After an event in South Carolina in 2015, I was completely spent, mentally and physically. My buddy Phillip McMillan was with me on the trip. I told him, "I'm worn out. I'm taking a hot shower and going to bed."

"Hey, let's go relax in the hot tub," he said.

"Ha! Hot tub," I said. "Naw."

Hey, I had a certain phobia about hot tubs. When I was a kid, we didn't have indoor plumbing in our log cabin home. There was a big tub outside, and my mother would fill it with hot water for us take a bath. Since I was the youngest boy, I was usually the last one to take a bath—after each of my older brothers: Jimmy Frank, Harold, Tommy, and Phil.

Hey, you wouldn't believe what they left in the water for me! They would play practical jokes on me every time. I'd find frogs, lizards, garter snakes, and fish in the tub. As soon as

I felt something crawling up my leg, I ran into the house in my birthday suit!

After we moved into a house with the luxury of indoor plumbing, I wasn't interested in taking a bath outside anymore. Nowadays, I'll jump into a swimming pool to cool off every once in a while, but only if I can see what is hanging out on the bottom. I've stayed away from hot tubs.

"What's a hot tub do?" I asked Phillip.

Hey, I'll admit I didn't know how a hot tub works. My nephew Willie has one at his house, and I'd seen him in it, but I assumed he was the one making the bubbles!

---

Willie has a hot tub at his house;
I assumed he was the one making the bubbles!

---

"It has high-powered jets and they're very relaxing," Phillip said. "You'll sleep like a baby after a few minutes in a hot tub."

I agreed to give it a try, and Phillip let me borrow a pair of his shorts. Security officers escorted us to a private hot tub, and we jumped in. Immediately, I felt relaxed. I could feel the jets working on the sore muscles in my back and legs. A sign next to the hot tub said we were supposed to use it for only twenty minutes, but we stayed for more than an hour.

By the time I climbed out of the hot tub, I was so relaxed that I could barely walk. Every muscle in my body was asleep! I could even hear my hamstrings snoring! I'm sure I looked pretty silly walking back to my room, holding up oversized shorts with one hand and my tea glass with the other.

Hey, I slept like a baby that night. I counted only three

cows jumping over a fence before I was snoring. I slept for twelve straight hours that night. The only reason I woke up was because Phillip was pounding on my door.

"Hey, that hot tub really made me relax," I said. "Every muscle in my body went to sleep and they're still asleep! I gotta get me one of those things."

When we returned home to West Monroe, Louisiana, I called my friend John Carter at the Pool Place. "John, bring me one of those hot tubs," I said.

John and his crew set up a hot tub on the back deck of my new house. Christine and I use it almost every day. It really helps us relax and wind down.

A few months after I purchased the hot tub, I was standing in the kitchen and saw thick black smoke coming from the woods behind our house. The fire was close enough to put my house in danger. I picked up the telephone and dialed 911.

"Hey, the woods behind my house are on fire," I said. "What on earth do I do?"

"Just take a deep breath, sir," the operator said. "Try to settle down and relax."

"Okay," I said, taking a few deep breaths. "I'm relaxed."

"Great," the operator said. "Where are you now?"

"I'm sitting in my hot tub with a glass of iced tea," I said.

*Share with the Lord's people who are in need.*

*Practice hospitality.*

—ROMANS 12:13 (NIV)

CHAPTER 3

# McMILLAN

Shortly after I moved back to West Monroe, Louisiana, from Alabama in 1999 to work for my brother Phil at Duck Commander, my nephews kept telling me I had to meet their friend Phillip McMillan.

Apparently, they had told Phillip a bunch of funny stories about me. Phillip started to wonder if the outrageous stories about their Uncle Si were really true or just more Robertson tall tales. Hey, my life story is kind of like *Forrest Gump*. I went to Vietnam. I run really fast. I like Dr Pepper. I'm a Ping-Pong champion. It might sound like a lot of fiction, but I promise, 95 percent is true! That's all I have to say about that.

When I met Phillip for the first time at a men's Bible study at his house, my nephews told me he was deaf in one ear. They told me I had to talk really loud because Phillip couldn't hear a thing. I was told he relied on lip reading to understand what others were saying. Of course, it wasn't true, but I believed them. Phillip's hearing was actually fine.

*Phillip McMillan (middle) is my right-hand man and best friend. He travels with me to events around the country, and my nephew Alan Robertson (right) also accompanies on occasion.*

Phillip also didn't know my nephews were playing a prank on us. For a couple of hours, I shouted in Phillip's face so he could read my lips, while he moved around trying to protect his personal space. Finally, my nephews and their buddies burst out laughing and told us about the prank. Hey, it was pretty funny.

Phillip and I quickly became close friends. If you've watched *Duck Dynasty,* you might remember Phillip playing the villain in a couple of episodes. In one show, he was portrayed as a nemesis of my nephews, and he and Willie raced on lawnmowers. In another episode, Jase and Phillip raced outhouses in a promotion for Willie's restaurant, Willie's Diner. And then he played dodgeball against my nephews in yet another episode. I have to say that Phillip, Jase, and Willie are actually close friends, and he has become my best friend. You'd have to search far and wide to find a better man. Phillip loves his wife and family and puts God before anything else.

---

I shouted in Phillip's face so he could read my lips, while he moved around trying to protect his personal space.

---

When *Duck Dynasty*'s popularity exploded, my family decided I needed to take a partner on the road with me for public appearances and charity events. Phillip and I were already close, so I told him he was going wherever I went. He calls himself the "Si Sitter." We have a close relationship that goes beyond business. We play cards together about once a week, hunt and fish together, and watch ball games together. We both love to laugh and cut up. In fact, my wife might be the only person who spends more time with me than Phillip.

As Phillip and I became closer friends, he started to share the story of his difficult past with me. His story reminded me a lot of my brother Phil, who battled his own demons before he became a follower of Jesus Christ. Like my brother, Phillip puts Jesus first and everything else second. He has become bold in his faith and isn't afraid to share the Gospel with others.

Phillip wasn't always that way, though. Each individual must make his or her own decision to follow the Almighty. Remember when Jesus asked the disciples who were with him this question: " 'Who do people say I am?' They replied, 'Some say John the Baptist, others say Elijah, and still others, one of the prophets.' 'But what about you,' he asked. 'Who do you say I am?' Peter answered, 'You are the Messiah' " (Mark 8:27–29).

That is the question Phillip had to answer when he was nineteen years old: Who is this Jesus Christ? Some of his friends said one thing and others said another, but Phillip had to ask himself what he believed to be true about Jesus, and whether he really knew Him.

At that point in Phillip's life, he really didn't know the Almighty. He knew of Him and had read about Him in the Bible, but the truth about Jesus didn't mean anything because Phillip was not yet ready to apply it to himself and his salvation. The truth was veiled to him. He was living in darkness.

Phillip had grown up in a happy family in West Monroe. He was close to his older brother, Danny, and his younger brother, Ricky. Phillip and his brothers grew up hunting and fishing with their father, Roy. His mother, Kathy, took them to church every Sunday morning when Phillip was young.

But when Phillip was twelve, his parents divorced. It was a shock to him and his brothers. They didn't understand why it was happening. Phillip lived with his friends for a while and really lashed out at his parents. He was bitter about their divorce and was too young to understand why it happened.

A few years later, Phillip's mother and father both remarried. He enjoyed spending time with each of them, but something inside him changed. Phillip felt like he couldn't trust anyone anymore. He feared that things could fall apart at any time. As a result, he decided not to ever let anyone get close to him again. He built walls around himself and guarded them well. In his mind, Phillip decided he would never be vulnerable again. He was alone.

Because of his isolation, Phillip started acting out. He was irresponsible and lived an immoral life. Drugs and alcohol became a regular part of his life, and he used them to mask his pain. He became selfish and didn't care if he hurt the people who loved him. In the back of Phillip's mind, he knew his bad decisions were probably going to kill him. He didn't care.

In fact there were many times when Phillip narrowly escaped death. When he was a teenager, he was the life of the party and willing to do anything to be the center of attention among his friends. One night at a party, Phillip climbed into the front seat of his buddy's new Ford Mustang GT, while another friend got into the back. They drove down a dark country road and came to a dead end. Phillip and his two friends in the car decided to find out how fast the Mustang would go. So they turned the car around and sped off.

A sharp curve was coming up in the road; Phillip looked at his buddy who was driving and saw the sweat on his face. Phillip knew his friend couldn't handle the turn, so he reached for his seat belt. As soon as it clicked, the car left the road, hit a culvert, and flipped. The next thing Phillip saw was flashing lights from police cars and ambulances. His two buddies suffered serious injuries and were transported to a hospital. Phillip only suffered a long scratch on his face and walked away from the wreck.

One of the sheriff's deputies at the accident scene told Phillip, "That seat belt saved your life. If you hadn't been wearing it, you would have been thrown through the windshield. You're lucky you're alive, son."

After another long night of partying, Phillip decided he was going to drive his truck to a hunting camp in Bosco, Louisiana, which is about twenty miles south of West Monroe. It was late at night, and Phillip shouldn't have been driving because he'd been drinking. Not far from the camp, he fell asleep and drove off the highway. His truck was headed straight for the Ouachita River. Miraculously, just before his truck reached the river, it got stuck in the mud. To add to that miracle, the side mirrors of his truck were wedged between two trees. These were the only things preventing the truck from falling over a cliff and into the river.

The next morning, Phillip's buddies heard the loud music from his truck's speakers. They found his truck stuck in the mud on the riverbank. He was asleep in the driver's seat and the engine was still running. Somehow, Phillip woke up alive that morning.

On another trip to his hunting camp in Bosco, Phillip and a couple of buddies stopped at a railroad crossing to relieve themselves. Phillip's buddy stopped his truck right on top of the tracks. Thankfully, Phillip came to his senses. "Man, if a train comes by, we're all going to die," Phillip told his buddies. A few minutes after Phillip moved the truck, a train came roaring past them. The engineer never blew the train's whistle because they were in the middle of nowhere.

There's no doubt about it: if Phillip hadn't turned his life around, he would have encountered an early grave. At one party, he passed out in a hot tub and nearly drowned. Fortunately, somebody walked by the hot tub and saw him underwater. Phillip was pulled out of the hot tub and spent the next several minutes coughing up water. On another night, a buddy dared Phillip to climb a five-hundred-foot tower. Somehow, even after consuming several beers, he managed to climb to the top and back down. Phillip still isn't sure how he pulled it off.

---

If Phillip hadn't turned his life around,
he would have encountered an early grave.

---

Even though Phillip was angry with God because of his parents' divorce and his difficult circumstances, he knew God was watching out for him. He believed God had a purpose and plan for him, but he wasn't willing to give his life to Jesus and find out what the Almighty had in store for him.

Fortunately, while Phillip pondered the truth about life and God, my nephew Jase shared the Good News with him. At first, Phillip and Jase didn't exactly jive. They both attended West Monroe High School but weren't close friends. Jase was living a straight-and-narrow life and didn't stray far from his Christian walk. Phillip, on the other hand, was hostile and angry toward God. He couldn't understand why his life was such a mess if God truly loved him. In many ways, Phillip and Jase were polar opposites. Jase knew of Phillip's reputation, which wasn't good. Jase didn't want much to do with Phillip, and vice versa.

When Phillip turned nineteen in January 1990, his good friend Blake Gaston told him that he'd changed his life and was never going back to his immoral life. Blake was one of Jase's good friends too. Blake told Phillip that Jase had shared the Gospel with him. Phillip was confused. Blake had been his wingman, and Phillip didn't understand what Jase could have told Blake that had made such a transformation in his life. It was such an abrupt and noticeable change.

Blake invited Phillip to attend a Bible study with him. Phillip was reluctant to go, but he was curious about hearing what had changed Blake's life. Phillip made Blake promise that he wouldn't draw any attention to him during the study. Phillip wanted to be a bystander and listen to what others were saying. He didn't want to talk about himself or his relationship with God.

A few days later, Phillip walked into the Bible study, and Jase immediately noticed him there.

"Phillip McMillan," Jase said to him, "do I have a story for you!"

Jase proceeded to share the Good News with Phillip. Jase explained that Phillip had three significant problems. First, he was disconnected from God. Sin had separated him from the Almighty. Second, Phillip was going to physically die one day, and he needed to be able to be physically raised from the grave in order to live eternally with God. Jase told Phillip that accepting Jesus Christ as his Lord and Savior was the only way to do it. Last, Jase told Phillip that even if he submitted to the Lord and became a Christian, he would eventually sin and need forgiveness and grace. Jesus could give him that too.

For the next hour, Jase told Phillip about how God became flesh in Jesus and sacrificed His life for us. Jase told him how Jesus was crucified, raised from the dead three days later, and then ascended into heaven to sit at God's right hand. Finally, Jase told him that because of Jesus' sacrifice, we are continuously cleansed of our sins if we accept Him as our Lord.

Phillip broke down in tears after Jase shared the Good News with him. He knew that what Jase was telling him was true. He'd read about it in the God-breathed scriptures of the Bible. Phillip made a life-changing decision to repent and was baptized that night. Phillip has told me many times that it was the greatest decision of his life. Phillip says Jase saved his life by sharing the Good News with him.

Phillip went home and told his girlfriend, Alicia Swan, about what he'd done. He wanted Alicia to talk to Jase as well. Alicia was the only girl Phillip had ever truly loved, and he wanted her to live a righteous life with him. He prayed so hard for God to bring Alicia to Him through her faith in Christ Jesus.

Phillip had known Alicia since grade school, but they didn't become friends until after they graduated from high school. She was one grade above Phillip, and he always believed she was out of his league. After they graduated, Alicia attended the University of Northeast Louisiana (it's now called the University of Louisiana–Monroe) and worked as an aerobics instructor at a fitness facility. Phillip was so in love with the girl that he signed up for her classes. For more than an hour, Phillip stretched, bent over, gyrated, and shook his buns. By the time he finally got his leotard on, the class was over!

After every class, Phillip would ask Alicia out on a date. She shot him down every time. After one of the classes, Phillip saw Alicia changing a flat tire on the side of the road. He stopped to help her, but she said she was fine and didn't need his assistance. In fact, Alicia told him she knew how to change a tire, change the motor oil, and fix anything else that could go wrong with a car. After hearing that, Phillip was even more in love with her. Despite her stubbornness, Phillip helped her anyway.

Finally, after Phillip sweated through another one of Alicia's aerobics classes, she told him how she really felt about him. "I know who you are," she said. "I have always known who you were. You're a jerk, and I don't want to date you!" How's that for letting a boy down gently? Phillip wasn't dejected, though. He set out to prove one thing to Alicia—that he wasn't a jerk.

_____

"I know who you are. I have always known who you were. You're a jerk, and I don't want to date you!"

_____

Through a friend, Phillip learned that Alicia was taking a class to renew her certification as an aerobics instructor. He decided he would register for the class. Phillip had no training in aerobics and is about as flexible as a cypress tree. But he sat next to her in every class and continued his courtship.

After a few weeks, Phillip finally persuaded Alicia to go to lunch with him. Then, after Phillip failed the aerobics class miserably, she agreed to go on a real date with him. "It's not because I like you," she told him. "It's because I feel sorry for you." Much to Alicia's surprise, Phillip made her laugh during the entire date.

Alicia and Phillip started dating seriously and were married on April 18, 1992. My nephew Alan presided over their wedding, and Jase said a prayer during the service. Even Phil was there. I think it's the first time I saw Phil at a wedding that didn't involve one of his boys. Phillip and Alicia now have three children: Bryson, nineteen; Blake, fifteen; and their little girl, Amber, fourteen.

I couldn't be prouder of Phillip. He and Jase went from polar opposites to close brothers in Christ and eventually, Phillip became a part of our family. He has led hundreds of people to the Lord through Bible studies with Phil, Jase, and Alan. He attended the School of Biblical Studies at White's Ferry Road Church in West Monroe. Jase and Alan also attended our church's seminary school, and my nephew Willie was in Phillip's class. Willie told Phillip about the first time he met him. Willie said Phillip pulled up next to him at a stop sign and waved a stack of hundred-dollar bills at him. Now, that's funny!

After graduating from seminary, Phillip attended Abilene Christian University in Abilene, Texas. He earned a bachelor's degree in Biblical Studies. He finished his master's degree in counseling at Northeast Louisiana University and has worked at the Louisiana Methodist Children's Home in Ruston since 1995. After working several years as a therapist, Phillip was hired as the home's director of admissions in 2002. He travels across Louisiana screening potential candidates for placement at homes. His group provides therapy and other services to more than twenty thousand patients and families most every year.

I've always believed that the Lord works in mysterious ways, and I think Phillip's difficult times as a teenager are the reason he is so successful at working with kids today. God had a hand in his life and had a purpose for him. Phillip's mission in life today is to help kids who are going through the same struggles he went through as a young man. It's pretty neat because he can use everything that happened in his life as lessons for the kids he counsels. With God's help, Phillip is helping them turn their lives around. It's an awesome thing to witness.

I'm happy God had mercy on Phillip. I'm happy Phillip finally realized God's purpose for his life. I'm thankful for the serenity and peace God has given my friend Phillip. I'm glad to see that families can work through divorce and still be a great example for the kingdom of God. I've had the privilege of meeting Phillip's extended family and must say they have been blessed. His mother, Kathryn, is one of the sweetest women I've ever met.

I believe that God causes certain people to come into our lives, and there is nothing more special than a Christian brother. As Proverbs 17:17 teaches us: *"A friend loves at all times, and a brother is born for adversity."* Our lives are not intended to be solo acts. We're not meant to be Lone Rangers.

# HALLU-SI-NATIONS
## Iced-Tea Cup

I'm not sure I ever would have made it through Vietnam without the care packages my mother sent me. I might have died from starvation. Hey, some of the food in the army wasn't that bad, but it was as bland as my nephew Willie's gumbo. Even worse, you couldn't find a jar of jalapeño peppers or a bottle of Tabasco within nine thousand miles of Can Tho to make the food taste better.

Fortunately for me, my mother, Merritt Robertson, took care of what I needed. In one of the first boxes, she mailed me a pair of work boots. Inside one of the boots was a Tupperware iced-tea cup and a couple of jars of jalapeño peppers; in the other one, she had put a couple of cans of SPAM and beans and wieners.

Somehow, Momma's iced-tea cup stayed with me for twelve months in Vietnam, and I've carried it in my back pocket ever since. I drink two gallons of iced tea a day, and my wife and I make it the old-fashioned way. It's the same way Moses made tea—Hebrewed it!

---

Momma's iced-tea cup stayed with me
for twelve months in Vietnam, and
I've carried it in my back pocket ever since.

---

We put three tea bags in a pot of water, turn on the heat on the stove, and let it boil. Then we put a lid on the pot and let it steep for about an hour. We pour the tea into a gallon jug, add cold water, and drink it. It's easy enough.

Hey, I only drink unsweetened iced tea. Hot tea is not my cup of tea, okay? People ask me all the time if I drink sweetened tea. I guess it's because I live in the South. I tell them, "Hey, I'm already sweet enough."

I even had a guy at the Country Music Awards ask me, "Hey, what proof is that tea?" I told him, "Hey, zero proof. I don't drink alcohol." Everybody thinks there's something else in my iced tea because I act funny, but that's just me. I promise I drink unsweetened tea, Jack!

Hey, iced tea cools you off and makes you feel good. I've also found that tea can settle a lot of disputes. If our world leaders would sit down and have a glass of iced tea together, I think we'd live in a much better place.

When my nephews were younger, they were pretty competitive and were constantly at one another's throats. It's the way most teenagers are. One day, Jep told me that he was fighting with his brothers. "Every night, Willie and Jase come home in a bad mood," he said. "They end up taking it out on me."

"Hey, here's what you do," I said. "When you hear their truck pull up, make yourself a big glass of iced tea. Then take the biggest gulp you can take, but don't swallow it until they go to bed."

A couple of days later, I saw Jep and asked him if it worked.

"Yeah, I did exactly what you said to do," he said. "I can't believe it worked."

"Hey, see what happens when you keep your mouth closed?" I said.

My iced-tea glass goes everywhere I go. It's either half full or half empty, depending on how my day is going. I prefer my original iced-tea glass, the one my momma sent me. But I do have a few backups in case something goes wrong.

One day, I was eating at a barbecue restaurant in Texas when my tea glass started leaking. I looked at the bottom and saw a crack. Apparently, I'd cracked it while getting it out of the cup holder of my truck.

I told the waitress, "Hey, would you please bring me another glass? This one seems to be leaking."

She looked at the cup in my hand and said, "Okay, what are you going to do with that one? Can I please have it?"

I signed the cup and gave it to her.

Another time, Christine's cat Sweet Pea knocked my empty cup off a side table and started chasing it around the room. Then she used the cup to sharpen her claws. Somehow the cat clawed a hole right through my cup!

There was one guy who even tried to buy my original cup. He handed me a blank check and said, "Fill in the amount. Whatever it takes—I want that Tupperware cup."

"Hey, it's not for sale," I told him.

The guy told me he'd give me six figures for the cup. I told him to go buy his own Tupperware cup, but he insisted he wanted mine. I told him the *Duck Dynasty* producers wouldn't let me sell it—it even said so in my contract.

Hey, when I was walking into the infield for the Duck Commander 500 at Texas Motor Speedway in April 2015, a security guard stopped me.

"Sir, we're going to have to confiscate your tea jug and iced-tea glass," he said. "You can't have those in here."

"Hey, you better call the president of the track," I said. "This glass and this jug are not departing my hands."

The guy got on his radio. A few minutes later, his cell phone rang. After a very short conversation, he hung up his phone.

"Mr. Robertson, have a nice day," he said.

That's what I'm talking about, Jack!

*There is a friend who sticks closer than a brother.*

—PROVERBS 18:24

CHAPTER 4

# PLANES, TRAINS, AND AUTOMOBILES

One of the great things about my job is that I get to travel all over the world to meet *Duck Dynasty* fans. I'm telling you, I have become one of the world's most sophisticated men.

During the past few years, I've been to Germany, Hawaii, Scotland, Mexico, and the Bahamas. I've traveled on cruise ships, private jets, high-speed trains, and helicopters. I've been to exotic places like Okeechobee, Florida; Spokane, Washington; and Des Moines, Iowa. Hey, the Dos Equis beer guy doesn't always travel, but when he does, he calls Silas Merritt Robertson for travel advice before he goes anywhere.

When we're not filming episodes of *Duck Dynasty* or hunting or fishing, I'm usually headed somewhere to speak at a church, college, or charitable organization. Being on the road isn't easy, and I'm sure glad I never had to work as a traveling salesman. I could have never made a living going

*You're probably not surprised to learn that taking a
nap is my favorite thing to do on an airplane.*

door-to-door trying to sell things like encyclopedias and
steak knives.

Hey, I'll never forget the time a vacuum cleaner salesman
showed up at our house when I was a kid. My momma answered the front door, and as soon as the salesman opened his
mouth, she said, "We don't have any money. I'm not interested."

But the salesman wedged his foot in the door so Momma couldn't close it.

"Hey, don't be so sure," he said. "After this demonstration, I promise that you'll want two of what I'm selling."

The salesman proceeded to dump a bag of fresh horse manure on the rug of our foyer.

"Ma'am, if this vacuum cleaner doesn't completely clean up this mess, I'll personally eat whatever is left," he said.

Momma looked at the poor guy and smiled.

"I hope you brought your appetite," she said. "They just cut off our electricity this morning."

Hey, it's never fun to travel alone, and one of my favorite things to do when I'm on the road is to embarrass my buddy Phillip McMillan, who goes with me just about everywhere. I get a big kick out of making Phillip look silly.

When we first started traveling all over the country, we took commercial flights. As you might imagine, we met thousands of people in airports and on planes. I always try to be humble and gracious with the fans. I'll take photos with them and sign autographs, especially for kids.

During a layover at Hartsfield-Jackson International Airport in Atlanta, I started taking photos and signing things, and it seemed like the line of fans lasted forever. Hey, it's the busiest airport in the world, Jack! After spending about an hour meeting people, somebody from the airline said, "Last call for Monroe, Louisiana." Well, I took off running for our gate and forgot all about my bags. Poor Phillip had to haul my luggage and his onto the plane. He barely made it onto the plane before the flight attendants closed the door.

"Hey, it's about time," I told him. "We were about to move this puppy on! By the way, did you get my bags?"

As my partner in crime, Phillip is in charge of making sure I have everything I need when we travel. On every trip, he makes sure to pack the following items for me: headrest, backup iced-tea cup (hey, you never know), Bible, deck of cards, Big League Chew, mosquito net, fork and spoon, and the latest copy of *Dog Fancy*. I won't go anywhere without that stuff.

Now, this might sound a little bit strange, but Phillip also keeps an empty Gatorade bottle on hand at all times. Hey, when you drink as much iced tea as I do, you never know when you're going to have to go, Jack! I've been in some tight spots while traveling, and that Gatorade bottle has saved me more times than I can count.

---

Phillip keeps an empty Gatorade bottle on hand at all times. When you drink as much iced tea as I do, you never know when you're going to have to go!

---

Over the years, my wife has been concerned about the amount of iced tea I drink every day. Other than a couple of glasses of water a day, it's the only thing I drink. Christine sent me to the doctor to make sure my kidneys were functioning okay.

"Well, how much iced tea do you actually drink?" the doctor asked me.

"About two gallons a day," I said.

"Is it sweet tea or unsweetened tea?" the doctor asked.

"Hey, it's unsweetened," I said. "I can't get any sweeter than I already am."

"Are you going to the bathroom regularly?" the doctor asked.

"I go about every thirty minutes," I said. "Thanks for asking."

"Well, it sounds to me like your kidneys are functioning quite well," he said. "In fact, your kidneys are probably functioning better than most people's."

That's why Phillip carries the empty Gatorade bottle. I never know when I'm going to have to go. When we're on a trip and the plane lands, the first thing I have to do is sprint for the restroom. I'm sure some of the people who have greeted us at airports have found me rather rude. Instead of shaking their hands and saying hello, I run by them to find the restroom.

Hey, one of the really nice things Phillip did for me to make traveling more enjoyable was to give me an iPod and headphones. He downloaded all of my favorite music onto it. I'll listen to about anything when I'm traveling, including Meatloaf and Korn. Hey, throw a little salt and pepper on it, and anything sounds good. I even like The Black Eyed Peas. The only problem: it makes me hungry when I say the name.

Now I listen to music whenever I'm on a plane. To be honest, I realized that when I have big headphones on my ears, no one seems to bother me. Don't get me wrong: I love talking to fans, but everybody needs peace and quiet every now and then. When you spend as much time as I do working in the Duck Commander reed room, where Jase, Jep, Godwin, and Martin are constantly running their mouths, it's nice to have some alone time every once in a while.

Before one of our flights, Phillip downloaded Luke Bryan's new album *Tailgates & Tanlines* on my iPod. My favorite song on the album is "Country Girl (Shake It for Me)." Well, I started listening to it during the flight, and I didn't realize I was singing it at the top of my lungs. I had those big headphones over my ears and couldn't hear myself. Everybody on the plane was laughing at me, including Phillip. He had his sunglasses on and was right there giggling with them. Now, whenever I see Phillip laughing at me because I'm singing, I sing even louder to embarrass him. Hey, I'm going to start charging admission on commercial flights. There isn't any such thing as a free show, Jack!

When we hit the road, it's usually only Phillip and me and maybe somebody else from *Duck Dynasty*. My wife, Christine, doesn't like to travel much, but she'll come with us every once in a while. A couple of years ago, I had an event in Virginia, and she decided to come along because our son, Scott, was still in the army and was living there. She wanted to see Scott, his wife, Marsha, and our four grandsons. Phillip's wife, Alicia, decided to make the trip with us as well.

Well, the plane ride to Virginia turned out to be pretty scary. Of course, I fell asleep within minutes of the plane taking off from Monroe. Christine was doing something on her iPad, and Alicia was listening to music on her iPod. About twenty minutes into the flight, Phillip heard loud noises.

Then one of the two pilots called him into the cockpit. Phillip couldn't believe what he saw: the plane's windshield was cracked. It looked like it was broken into one thousand pieces.

"The pressure cracked the windshield," the pilot said. "The good news is it's a double-paned windshield. The bad news is they're both cracked. We're going to have to turn the plane around. Make sure everybody is buckled up. This could get a little bumpy, so keep everybody calm."

Phillip went back to his seat and told Christine and Alicia what happened. Phillip thought to himself, *This is it. It's really over.* The hair on the back of his neck was even standing up. Christine could sense that Phillip was nervous.

"Phillip, honey, calm down," Christine told him. "Everything is going to be fine. Trust in the Lord and have no fear. If it's our time, it's our time. Either way, we'll be okay because God is in control."

---

Phillip was as nervous as a long-tailed cat
on the front porch of a Cracker Barrel.

---

Hey, Phillip was the one who was supposed to be keeping everyone else calm, but he was as nervous as a long-tailed cat on the front porch of a Cracker Barrel. It was Christine who was making him feel at peace. Finally, Phillip decided to wake me from my nap and tell me what was happening. I woke up and looked at the windshield. Phillip told me pressure cracked it.

"Naw, a bird hit the windshield," I told him.

"Si, if a bird hit the windshield, the pilots would have seen it happen," Phillip said.

"Hey, it was a bird," I told him. "It was probably a duck!"

I went back to sleep. Phillip texted my nephew Jase when the plane was at low enough altitude to get a cellular signal on his phone. He wrote: "Hey, we might not make it. Thanks for sharing the Gospel with my family and me. Pray for us. Love you, Bro."

Of course, the plane landed safely back in Monroe, or I wouldn't be sitting here telling you the story. When the plane stopped on the runway, Christine, Phillip, and I held hands and said a prayer, in which we thanked the Almighty for protecting us. It was a close call. Jase told us later that he was playing golf with his brother Alan when he received Phillip's text message. He told Alan, "What is Phillip talking about? He and Si are up to something!" It was typical Jase.

Hey, driving to events can sometimes be more hazardous than flying. One time, I rode with Jep and his wife, Jessica, to a small town in Texas. It was my turn to drive, and I might have been going a few miles over the speed limit because we were running late. A Texas State Trooper pulled us over on Interstate 10 near Houston.

In Louisiana, when the state police stop you, you're supposed to get out the car and walk back to the trooper. I think they do it to make sure the driver doesn't have a gun, and because they don't want the trooper walking on the side of a busy interstate. Well, that's apparently not how it works in Texas. When I got out of our car and started to walk back to the trooper's car, he and his partner jumped out with their guns drawn!

"Put your hands in the air and show us your license and registration," one of the troopers said.

"Hey, I don't want to move," I told them. "You guys have your guns drawn on me and they're cocked!"

Thankfully, we worked things out. They wrote me a warning, and we went on down the road. God bless Texas.

Hey, there was another time when my sister-in-law Kay and I were driving to a book signing in Arkansas. After a couple of hours, we made a pit stop to use the restroom. I got back into the car and drove about twenty miles down the road. Suddenly, I saw a county sheriff in my rearview mirror. He was coming at me fast. He pulled next to me, flipped his lights on, and pulled me over.

He walked up to my window and said, "Hey, did you know that you left your sister-in-law at the gas station?"

"Thank the Good Lord," I said. "I thought I'd gone deaf."

To be honest, I would much prefer to travel to a small town than a big city. Don't get me wrong: I've met thousands of nice people in big cities like Dallas, Las Vegas, Los Angeles, Milwaukee, New York, and San Antonio, Texas. Hey, they're proud of their cities and love living there. It's great they feel that way. I only know that I couldn't be surrounded by all of that asphalt, concrete, and noise. I much prefer living out in the country, and the people who live in small towns seem to be a lot more like me.

I'll never forget the first time I visited New York for a *Duck Dynasty* promotion. To be honest, I wasn't thrilled about having to go to the Big Apple, even though I think everyone should visit every big US city at least once. We were staying in a hotel near Central Park, and I couldn't believe what we were paying for our rooms. The hotel was charging us about one thousand dollars per night! It was highway robbery!

When we arrived at the hotel, a bellman grabbed my bags out of our limousine. I checked in at the front desk, and the bellman told me he would take me to my room. When he opened the door, my jaw dropped to the floor. It was the smallest hotel room I'd ever seen. It didn't even have a bath-room!

"Hey, Jack, I was born at night—but not last night!" I told him. "You're not charging me one thousand dollars a night for this closet."

"Sir, this is the elevator," he said.

Look, if you can get used to the hustle and bustle of big cities, they're not bad places to visit. I only know that I wouldn't want to live in any of them. I had a great time in New York. I saw the Statue of Liberty, Times Square, Broadway, the 9/11 Memorial, the Empire State Building, the diner where Jerry Seinfeld ate, and Yankee Stadium. It ended up being a very fun and educational experience. Hey, I saw plenty of strange things in New York, but I'm not going to get into that.

I'm telling you: you wouldn't believe some of the odd things I've seen during my travels. I saw the world's largest brick in Montgomery, Alabama. I saw the world's largest jack-in-the-box in Middletown, Connecticut; the biggest ball of twine in Canker City, Kansas; and the largest bottle of catsup in Collinsville, Illinois. I'll never forget seeing the world's biggest ball of stamps in Boys Town, Nebraska. Hey, if you think putting reeds in millions of duck calls is repetitive work, try licking all of those suckers, Jack!

It drives Phillip nuts when I make him go two hours out of the way so I can see something odd. I've had my photo taken with Lenny the Chocolate Moose in Scarborough, Maine; Lucy the Elephant in Margate City, New Jersey; and the Giant Peach in Gaffney, South Carolina. When I'm going to speak at a small town, I like to learn as much as possible about where I'm going. For whatever reason, I'm really attracted to oddities and unique landmarks.

---

For whatever reason, I'm really attracted to oddities and unique landmarks.

---

Now, let me tell you about the strangest thing I ever saw while we were on the road. We were driving to an appearance in Jackson, Mississippi, and we stopped for gas shortly after we crossed the state line. It was a nice, sunny afternoon during the summer, and I noticed a couple of guys digging holes on the side of the road. It was the strangest sight: one guy would dig a hole and then the other guy would fill it behind him. The first guy probably dug four holes and then the second guy filled them while I was watching.

After I paid for our gas and bought a bag of ice for my tea, my curiosity got the best of me. I walked down to the side of the road where the guys were digging holes.

"Hey, what are y'all doing?" I asked them. "Why are you digging holes if he's only going to fill them back up with dirt?"

One of the guys looked at me and said, "Well, there's usually three of us. I dig a hole, Larry puts a post in it, and then Dave puts dirt on top of it. Larry's out sick, but that doesn't mean we can't work today."

Hey, Jack, I jumped back in the truck with Phillip, and we headed down the road. I wasn't about to catch what those boys had.

Some of the nicest people I've ever met were in small towns. Maybe it's because they look and talk like me, but I seem to relate to them better. I'll never forget when we stopped in a one-stoplight town in the middle of Texas. I really had to use the restroom and was nearly dying of hunger, so we stopped at a café on Main Street. I'm pretty sure it was the only restaurant in town.

When Phillip and I walked into the café, there were probably fifty people in there waiting to order their lunch. When they saw me, the place went dead silent. I turned around to see if Dallas Cowboys quarterback Tony Romo was standing behind me. Within minutes, people were lining up to shake my hand and take a photo with me. When I was finished, we got our plates and sat and ate lunch with the whole group. It felt like we were sitting at our dinner table at home, as we shared stories and told jokes with one another.

During another trip, we stopped at a barbecue joint in

Oklahoma. When it was our turn to order our food at the cash register, the lady looked at me and said, "Did anybody ever tell you that you look like Uncle Si?"

"Hey, every day of my life," I told her.

Once she figured out that it was actually me, I signed autographs and took photos with everybody in the restaurant. I loved every second of it. When I was finished, Phillip and I went to a back room in the restaurant. We sat at a table with an older man and his wife. We must have talked with them for an hour, and they loved on us and shooed people away from our table while we were eating. We felt so much at home.

Hey, that's what I love about small-town USA. Everybody knows everybody, and no one is a stranger. I don't know what it is, but people seem to be friendlier and more inviting. In small towns, there is plenty of fresh air and open parking spaces. You can see the stars at night, and, hey, if you look hard enough you might even see a billy goat standing on top of a bull. Hey, I've actually seen it happen in thirteen states.

*Be kind and compassionate to one another.*

—Ephesians 4:32 (NIV)

# CHAPTER 5

# WOUNDED WARRIORS

After living nearly seven decades on earth, I know one thing for certain: there's nothing like having peace of mind when you lay your head on a pillow every night. It's a rare commodity.

Hey, I like to nap as much as anyone. In fact, some days I'll nap six or seven times. But I have to admit that sometimes at night I lie in bed with so much garbage in my mind it's like there's a runaway train inside my head. When this happens, I can't stop it. On those nights, I know sleep will never come—this was especially true in Vietnam.

My son, Scott, was deployed three times to Iraq while serving in the United States Army. I can't imagine what he went through or what pain those events cause him even now. He spent three years of his life away from his family. Some servicemen and servicewomen are being deployed to the Middle East for seven years to help us fight the global war on terror. Depending on what these men and women endured during the war, what they had to do and what they saw, they're going to struggle to have peace of mind. They spent many years of their lives in war, Jack!

I can't imagine the junk that would be in my head if I spent my days dodging roadside bombs, suicide bombers, and mortar shells. Hey, when you're over there, you never know who is going to try to ambush you. Maybe it's a young boy with grenades in his hands. Maybe it's a woman with a bomb under her dress. You never know where the next attack is going to come from. It's a tough circumstance to live with any way you slice it.

If you read my first book, *Si-cology 1: Tales and Wisdom from Duck Dynasty's Favorite Uncle,* you might remember the story about Scott's early life. He was born at a military hospital at Lackland Air Force Base in San Antonio, Texas, on December 18, 1977. Scott was born seven weeks premature because Christine suffered hemorrhaging and doctors couldn't stop her bleeding. The births of both of my children were miracles. Doctors told Christine that she'd never have children because of a serious medical condition. That's the reason she rejected my proposal for marriage so many times—until my charm and good looks finally won her over.

When Scott was born, doctors weren't even sure he would survive more than a few weeks. Fortunately, Scott weighed five pounds, thirteen ounces at birth, so he was bigger than most premature babies. When Scott was three days old, doctors operated on him because his liver wasn't functioning properly. The operation and a blood transfusion saved his life. There's no doubt in my mind that the Almighty was watching over him and us. I didn't know it then, but as Scott got a little older, we were going to need His strength and peace to guide us through the storm.

———

When Scott was born, doctors weren't even sure
he would survive more than a few weeks.

———

Years later, we learned that Scott's early health problems had damaged his brain. He was suicidal from the time he was about five years old. His behavior was erratic and often violent. He lashed out at his mother and me, and damaged anything he could get his hands on when he was angry. When Scott was eleven years old, Christine stopped him from jumping out of a second-story window in our apartment. I'm not sure if the fall would have killed him, but it was clear that our son needed serious medical help.

The next day, we took Scott to see an army psychiatrist, who diagnosed him with attention disorder, behavioral disorder, and hyperactivity. The doctor prescribed Scott new medication, and his behavior changed almost immediately. He became a sweet, loving boy and was a joy to be around. We later learned that Scott was actually suffering from Asperger's syndrome, which is a form of autism.

Scott graduated from Paint Rock Valley High School in Princeton, Alabama, in 1996. We were living there after I retired from the military. That summer, while Scott was visiting his sister, Trasa, in Texas, he enlisted in the army without our blessing. His mother and I weren't especially thrilled with what he'd done, but we were going to support him as he started a military career.

Scott wanted to be a soldier from the time he was a kid. For whatever reason, he wanted to be like his dad. Christine and I tried to talk him into pursuing another occupation, but it's the only thing he ever wanted to do. To be honest, we hoped his medical history would prevent him from enlisting.

Scott joined the army and went to basic training at Fort Jackson in Columbia, South Carolina, in November 1997. He completed advanced individual training at Fort Eustis in Virginia. Scott and Marsha now have four boys—Ethan, twins Connor and Logan, and Wyatt. Ethan was Marsha's son from her first marriage, and Scott adopted him. The boys had to live without their father while he was away, which was a huge sacrifice for them and their mother.

Scott's first deployment to Iraq was from April 1, 2003, to March 1, 2004. The year 2004 was very difficult for Scott. His grandfather died that year, and I came close to dying with my heart attack. And the most difficult of all was the death of his first wife. Without any counseling for his previous deployment or for his family losses, Scott was deployed to the Middle East on December 1, 2005, and didn't come back until November 17, 2006. He went back again on June 14, 2008, and finally came home for good on June 4, 2009.

Every day Scott was gone, Christine and I prayed to the Lord to bring our son home safe. Talk about not having peace of mind. There's nothing worse than worrying about your child every minute of every day, Jack! It was the worst three years of my life. I didn't know if I was going to get a knock at the door from two men in uniform who were there to tell us that our son had been killed in action. It's an awful experience too many families have endured.

After Scott's last deployment, he left active combat and became an army recruiter. He and his family moved next door to us in West Monroe in May 2014. After Scott was so far away from us for so long, it's good to have him and his family close to us now. His kids are such a joy to be around.

I rarely talked to Scott about what he did or what he saw while he was serving in Iraq. I can only imagine what happened to him over there. Among other things, he served as a crew chief on helicopters. His unit transported injured soldiers and prisoners of war, as well as conducting air assaults and numerous other types of missions. It was very dangerous work, but the Good Lord made sure he was safe.

From what I could tell, Scott was adjusting fine to civilian life after he moved to West Monroe. He is a great dad to his four sons and is very active in their lives. He is a wonderful husband and loves his wife dearly. He seemed to be enjoying his new career as an army recruiter. I couldn't be prouder of the man he has become.

But in August 2015, his PTSD manifested itself in a significant way. One afternoon, Scott stopped to help a homeless man on the side of the road. After taking the man to breakfast, Scott dropped him off where he had found him. Then Scott went home and got his family for a meal at the local Olive Garden restaurant. On the way home, Scott began driving erratically, missing familiar turns and being very distracted. Marsha kept asking Scott if he was okay, and he would tell her yes. She finally told him that one of the boys needed a bathroom break, and after the stop, she convinced him to let her drive. As Marsha drove into their driveway, Scott collapsed like a puppet without strings.

I hadn't realized before that day how much the PTSD was affecting Scott and what it was putting Marsha through. Marsha called me after they got home, and I went to their house and helped Marsha get Scott out of the car. It was as if he wasn't even there. I've never been so scared in my life. I couldn't tell if Scott was even hearing what I was saying to him. I stayed with him for about forty-five minutes and he finally came around. "Dad," he told me, "I was deployed for thirty-six months and don't remember anything at all about that time."

The next day, Marsha took Scott to see an army psychiatrist. The doctor asked Scott about seeing the homeless man on the street. Scott said the man reminded him of some of the prisoners he encountered in Iraq. The man's face was dirty, his clothes were tattered, and he was malnourished. He looked like many of the handcuffed prisoners who were in Scott's helicopters.

The episode that day triggered Scott's PTSD and took him back to Iraq. Scott had been seen by army doctors since 2010, but the only diagnosis he had been given was the catch-all diagnosis of "anxiety disorder, otherwise unspecified." Fortunately, after this panic attack, Scott was finally diagnosed with PTSD and is now getting the medical care he needs. Scott still suffers from anxiety, and I'm sure he has endured many sleepless nights. But he's getting better with the help of his doctors and his family.

It really angers me that we don't do more for our veterans, who are America's real heroes. I didn't actually see any combat in Vietnam, but I was over there and was at risk too. Anyone who has worn the uniform and was in a foreign country at a time of war was in danger. We lost more than 58,000 service men during the Vietnam War. Unfortunately, we have lost additional men to suicide after they came home from Vietnam. It's one of our country's greatest embarrassments. To be honest, it's really shameful that we don't do more. For the life of me, I can't understand why our government will do more for people who don't want to help themselves than for the people who are putting themselves in danger every day to protect our country.

It really angers me that we don't do more for our veterans, who are America's real heroes.

Post-traumatic stress disorder wasn't even recognized until after the Vietnam War, and so, many veterans didn't get the mental health care they needed when they came home. Our government didn't do enough to help them cope with the horrors they witnessed during a truly awful struggle.

In 2012 alone, the Department of Veterans Affairs reported that it treated 476,515 veterans for PTSD—most of them veterans of the Vietnam War almost fifty years ago. Tragically, those women and men didn't have access to the kind of mental health services they needed when they returned home. They've been suffering from the effects of war for more than a half century. Imagine having to live with those memories each and every day.

Unfortunately, we're going through the same tragic situation now. More than 2.4 million Americans have served in Afghanistan, Iraq, and other parts of the world during the global war on terror since the September 11, 2001, attacks on America. More than 600,000 of them are struggling with PTSD and major depression. The VA has formally diagnosed more than 200,000 Iraq and Afghanistan veterans with having PTSD. Another 400,000 service members have been diagnosed with a traumatic brain injury they received in combat.

Tragically, even more women and men are suffering from those conditions who haven't yet been properly diagnosed. They're continuing to live with the horrors of being shot at, seeing dead bodies, being attacked and ambushed, and taking mortar fire. Some are suffering from survivor guilt after seeing their buddies wounded or killed. Hey, we have to get them the help they desperately need, regardless of the financial costs. It's the least we can do for the men and women fighting for our freedom every day. During the last few years, helping the men and women who fought for our country has become one of my greatest causes. There's no question the Good Lord has blessed my family mightily. Because of the popularity of *Duck Dynasty,* we now have the financial means and public spotlight to make a difference in important causes. Helping wounded veterans and their families is a cause that is very important to me.

In 2014, I was asked to appear in the movie *Faith of Our Fathers,* a faith-based film that sought not only to honor Vietnam veterans but also to help them and their families heal from the wounds of being forgotten. The film was produced by Pure Flix, which has also released faith-based movies like *God's Not Dead* and *Do You Believe?* Hey, if you haven't noticed, there aren't a lot of good messages coming out of Hollywood these days. I was honored to be a part of a film that shared the Gospel and honored men and women who truly deserve it.

*Faith of Our Fathers* is the story of two strangers whose fathers were killed in Vietnam. One of the men is a man of great faith, while the other is a doubtful cynic because of his father's premature death. Together, they use their fathers' handwritten letters from the battlefield to search for clues about how they died. Their journey eventually takes them to the Vietnam Veterans Memorial in Washington, D.C. I played the role of a gas station clerk in the film. Actors Candace Cameron Bure and Stephen Baldwin also were in the movie.

*Faith of Our Fathers* was released in July 2015, which commemorated the fiftieth anniversary of the Vietnam War. I appeared at advance screenings around the country and had the pleasure of meeting thousands of Vietnam veterans. They're my brothers-in-arms, Jack. I know what they went through over there and what they're going through now. On the last advanced screening in West Monroe, I was presented with a fiftieth anniversary flag from the US Department of Defense. It was a great honor, and I accepted the flag on behalf of Vietnam veterans everywhere, including the thousands of men who died over there.

So many young men went to Vietnam and didn't come home. There are a lot of sons and daughters who never really got to know their dads and moms, which is truly tragic. It happens in all wars. Hopefully, in a small way, *Faith of Our Fathers* helped bring some peace to people who are still hurting from that awful war.

In December 2015, I was honored to join my brother Phil, his wife, Kay, and their sons, Alan and Jep, at Operation Heal Our Patriots in Port Alsworth, Alaska. Samaritan's Purse, a Christian-based ministry founded by Bob Pierce in 1970, invites one hundred and fifty couples to their retreat center every year. The lodge is located on the shores of Hardenburg Bay in the southwestern portion of Lake Clark National Park and Preserve. It's one of the most beautiful places I've seen, and it's only accessible by small plane.

Former Alaska governor Sarah Palin and her husband, Todd, were also there to help us greet the ten service members and spouses who were attending the retreat that week. Together, we stood on the runway waving American flags when the service members arrived. It was very special for me to be there because these veterans never received a proper homecoming. They were injured in combat and were transported back to military hospitals in the US. Nobody threw

*I had the pleasure of meeting former Alaska governor Sarah Palin
and her husband, Todd, when I visited veterans at Operation
Heal Our Patriots, a ministry of Samaritan's Purse.*

them a ticker-tape parade or properly thanked them for their
service when they came home, which they certainly deserved.
Hey, we send them over there to fight. The least we can do is
show our appreciation when they come home.

I can't thank Samaritan's Purse enough for the good work
it is doing for our military members. The wounded veterans
who are invited to Operation Heal Our Patriots spend one
week attending faith-based seminars to strengthen their re-

lationships with God and their marriages. During the week I went to the Samaritan Lodge in 2015, five people were baptized and six couples rededicated their marriages. Now, that's the Good Lord at work, Jack!

---

We send them over there to fight. The least we can do is show our appreciation when they come home.

---

Samaritan's Purse is one of my favorite ministries. Franklin Graham, the son of spiritual leader Billy Graham, has served as president and chief executive officer of Samaritan's Purse since 1979. The ministry meets the needs of the poor, sick, and suffering people in more than one hundred countries around the world. I've teamed up with Samaritan's Purse in other projects, including Operation Christmas Child, which collects shoe boxes filled with Christmas gifts and necessities for needy children. Samaritan's Purse is a great organization and is very visible evidence of the Almighty's extraordinary work.

Being a veteran myself, I was happy to be welcoming veterans home. I never had a homecoming when I came back from Vietnam. It was a controversial war, and most Americans didn't think we should be fighting someone else's war in a faraway land. Hey, I didn't have a choice in whether or not I went to Vietnam. Uncle Sam drafted me, and I spent one year in Southeast Asia, whether I wanted to be there or not,

Jack! Fortunately, I wasn't abused when I came home, like other Vietnam veterans.

It really sickens me when I see how some veterans are treated in this country, even today. Members of the Westboro Baptist Church in Topeka, Kansas, protest at servicemembers' funerals around the country. That isn't a church; it's a hate organization. Men and women are coming home in coffins, and they decide to picket at their funerals, where people are burying their sons, daughters, mothers, fathers, husbands, and wives. Hey, Jack, they were overseas fighting for your freedom of speech, whether you're wrong or right. He or she died for the right for you to run your mouth. It's disrespectful to the fallen soldiers and our country!

I know one thing: I'll continue to honor our servicemen and servicewomen until the day they put me six feet under the ground. Every time I see a soldier in an airport or at one of my charity events, I make sure to stop and shake his or her hand and thank them for their service. Hey, it's the least I can do for what they and their families have sacrificed for you and me. I can't thank them enough for putting their lives on the line to protect America. Some gave all. All gave some. We should never forget that, Jack!

# HALLU-SI-NATIONS

## Horses

Hey, I've never been much of a horse guy. We had horses on our farm when I was growing up, but they were working horses. My daddy used them to plow fields and our vegetable gardens, and my siblings and I never rode them. We cared for the horses, like feeding them, brushing them, and cleaning their stalls, but I wouldn't say they were our pets.

I've only ridden a horse once. It was such a terrifying experience that I never saddled one again. When I was about seven years old and shopping with my mom, I rode a horse for the first time. Once I was in the saddle, I put my feet in the stirrups and grabbed the reins. The first few minutes were fine. The horse trotted along, and the ride was actually pretty enjoyable.

But when I loosened my grip on the reins, it was like I'd unleashed a wild bronco. The horse took off! I was so terrified that I put my arms around the horse's neck. I fell off the side, but the horse kept going. Fortunately, my feet were still in the stirrups, or my head might have been bouncing off the ground. My momma screamed for help as she watched in horror.

All of the sudden, a cashier came running out of the department store where we were shopping and unplugged the horse. Hey, she probably saved my life. It was a close call.

Since I'm still afraid to ride horses, I figured I'd buy one that somebody else could ride. I thought it might be fun, and maybe I could make some money with my investment. Hey, do you know how you make a small fortune from horses? By starting with a large fortune, Jack! At least they're cheaper to shoe than my wife, Christine!

Do you know how you make a small fortune from horses? By starting with a large fortune, Jack!

In February 2014, I became part owner of a filly named Sithechristmas Elf (read, Si the Christmas Elf). Ashley Howard Nelson, who is Korie Robertson's sister, is also a part owner of the horse, along with Wes Melcher, who operates Double Infinity Ranch in Sulphur Springs, Texas.

*I've always had a way with animals, especially horses.*
*Do you like horses? Yay or neigh?*

Now, you would probably think that a horse named after me would be pretty fast. Well, that's not exactly true.

Sithechristmas Elf was bred in Louisiana and was two years old when we bought her—she was still a work in progress.

Unfortunately, she finished next to last in her first race at the Fair Grounds Race Course in New Orleans on January 30, 2015. Hey, our horse was so slow our jockey could have kept a diary of the race. There might have been a photo finish for last place, but it was too dark by the time they finally finished.

After that inauspicious start to her racing career, Sithechristmas Elf ran seven more races in 2015. She had a second-place finish at Evangeline Downs in Opelousas, Louisiana. Hey, maybe there is hope for her yet. I really think the only thing she needs is a good motivational speech. They don't call me the Horse Whisperer for nothing.

Now, there is actually another racehorse named after me that is much faster than the one I own. Go figure, Jack. George "Chip" McEwen and Anthony Robertson own a New York–bred horse named Uncle Sigh.

I really like what they're doing. McEwen was on a flight with his girlfriend in 2011 when the pilot asked everyone to remain seated until a wounded veteran could depart the plane. The young man had lost most of his motor skills after being hit by an IED.

McEwen was so moved by the incident that he renamed his ranch Wounded Warrior Stables in honor of military veterans injured or killed in Afghanistan. He donates 10 percent of his horses' earnings to various charities that support injured veterans, including Retrieving Freedom, which trains dogs to assist soldiers suffering from post-traumatic stress disorder.

Uncle Sigh has turned out to be his best horse. In his second career start, on December 27, 2013, he won the race by fourteen and a half lengths at Aqueduct Racetrack in Queens, New York. In fact, Uncle Sigh finished first or second in each of his first four starts. He looks like one of the most promising racehorses in America.

On May 3, 2014, Uncle Sigh finished fourteenth in the Kentucky Derby, the most famous horse race in the world. His silks were yellow and purple and depicted a purple heart. After racing in the Run for the Roses, Uncle Sigh finished in the top five in four races in 2015, including his second victory at Aqueduct Racetrack.

Hey, it makes me proud to have my name on a horse that helps raise awareness about wounded veterans and their charities.

*May you rejoice in the wife of your youth.*

—PROVERBS 5:18 (NIV)

# CHAPTER 6

# MY SMOKIN' HOT HONEY

It seems like every spring the past few years the producers of the TV show *The Bachelor* have called me. Some guy or gal from Hollywood will be on the other end of the phone, and he or she always ask me the same question: "Mr. Robertson, we're putting together our show for next season. We wanted to make sure you're still married because we think you would make a great bachelor."

"Yep, I'm still married," I'll tell them.

Hey, I don't get a lot of joy in breaking their hearts. Between the TV producers and the magazine editors that compile their annual lists of America's most eligible bachelors, I try to let them down easy.

It's not like I'm trying to hide the fact that I'm married. When I go grocery shopping, I sometimes pick up a dozen roses and some candy for my wife, Christine. From time to time, I remind her of how much she means to me. When I get to the checkout line, the lady at the cash register always says, "You're such a good husband."

*After forty-three years of marriage, me and my smokin' hot honey, my wife, Christine, renewed our vows during a ceremony in May 2014.*

"Hey, you can tell I'm married because of what I'm buying?" I ask her.

"No, it's because you're so good-looking," she says.

While I was kidding about *The Bachelor* and the magazines, it still surprises me how many women who watch *Duck Dynasty* don't know I'm married. No matter how hard I try, a lot of female fans still think I'm single.

Christine has never appeared on the show. From the start, she didn't want anything to do with being on reality TV. She said living with me was as much reality as she needs. Plus, her health won't allow her to be a part of the show. Filming episodes of *Duck Dynasty* might last several weeks, and we're often working eight to ten hours a day. It isn't easy, Jack! I guess that's why women think I'm single. Over the past few years, several women have proposed to me during my speaking engagements and other public appearances. My brother Phil can't understand why women find me so attractive. He says, "I'd understand it if they wanted to marry Willie because he has all the money. I'd even understand it if they wanted to marry Jase because he's Willie's right-hand man. But, no, they want to marry that—that goat!"

---

I was a player before they even invented the game, Jack!

---

Hey, I'm willing to give Phil the benefit of the doubt. He wasn't around me much when I was younger because I spent so much time in the military. He didn't see the effect Silas Merritt Robertson had on women when I was in my prime. Hey, they were on me like bees on a honeypot! I was a player before they even invented the game, Jack!

I still have that effect on certain women. I'll never forget the time a lady waited in line for hours to meet me. She was with a couple of her friends, and when they arrived at the front of the line, she popped the question.

"I want you to marry me," she said.

"Hey, you don't have enough money for me to marry you," I told her.

"Hold on," she said.

Then she brought her friends to the table where I was sitting.

"Hey, tell him how much I'm worth," she said.

"If you lived to be a hundred years old, you couldn't spend all of her money," one of the ladies said.

"Well, then we've got a problem," I said.

"What's the problem?" she asked.

"I've got a little redhead at home who won't like it," I told her.

Some of the other women who have proposed to me have been a little more direct. They've sent photographs of themselves in love letters to our house. What they don't know is that Christine is the one who actually reads their letters, and she has responded not so kindly to a few of them. Hey, what can I say? When you've got it, you've got it, Jack!

In spite of all the attention I get from women I meet on the road, the Good Lord has filled my heart with love and loyalty for my own Hot Honey. His peace and His power is the anchor of my heart and soul.

After more than four decades of marriage, I'm convinced there is someone out there for everybody. If you've seen my nephews, you'd know that's certainly the case. I tried to warn Korie, Missy, and Jessica about my nephews, but they wouldn't listen. I told the girls that Jase, Jep, and Willie are a lot like lawnmowers. They're hard to get started, they emit toxic fumes, and they only work half the time!

My nephews weren't the only ones who out-punted their coverage when it comes to marriage. The former Christine Raney and I met shortly after I left Vietnam on October 17, 1969. The army transferred me to Fort Devens in Shirley, Massachusetts, which is about fifty-five miles northwest of Boston. I was stationed there for about two years and worked in medical supply.

Christine was born and raised in Kentucky, where her father was a farmer. She was working as a seamstress in a factory that made furniture upholstery when I met her. One night, she and two of her friends picked me up when I was hitchhiking to an off-base nightclub in November 1969. From the start, Christine didn't like me much—she thought I was arrogant and full of myself. And maybe I was.

About a month later, one of Christine's friends set me up with her on a blind date to our company's Christmas party. Christine thought the date was going to be a disaster, but I charmed her with my humor and dancing skills. We ended up having a great time. We dated seriously for about two years, and when my enlistment was about to end, I was ready to propose to her. I knew I was going to move back to Louisiana to be closer to my family, and I really wanted Christine to come with me.

On April Fools' Day 1971, I told Christine's best friend

that I was going to ask her to marry me. I was only kidding at the time, but five days later, I really did pop the question—and she told me no. In fact, she rejected my proposal at least ten times. Christine didn't want to marry me because she knew how much I loved children. She had been previously married, and her first husband left her because she didn't think she could have children because of an underlying medical condition.

"Hey, I know someone, and by that I mean the Almighty," I told her. "If God wants us to have children, then we'll have children."

Well, my pleading finally won Christine over and we were married on April 7, 1971, by the justice of the peace at the courthouse in Berlin, Massachusetts. I was so poor that I couldn't buy her an engagement ring or wedding band, so during the ceremony, I put a cigar band on her finger.

---

I was so poor that I couldn't buy her an engagement ring or wedding band, so during the ceremony, I put a cigar band on her finger.

---

"Hey, look, put the cigar band on your finger," I told her. "It's what we say to each other that matters, not what you put on your finger."

While you ladies wipe away the tears from your eyes, let me tell the men out there how to keep a marriage intact for forty-five years. Keep your mouth closed and your checkbook open, boys! A cigar band really *isn't* enough! It didn't take me long to realize that marriage puts a ring on a woman's finger and two rings under the man's eyes. Hey, in India the men don't know their wives until the day they're married. Let me tell you something: that's the case everywhere in the world, Jack!

Joking aside, Christine and I have enjoyed a wonderful life together. We've been married for nearly a half-century, and we've lived in Alabama, Kentucky, Louisiana, North Carolina, and Texas. We even spent parts of seven years living in Germany while I was stationed there with the army.

Despite Christine's initial concerns about not being able to have children, the Lord blessed us with two wonderful kids. Our daughter, Trasa, was born in Landstuhl, Germany, on August 30, 1975, and our son, Scott, was born at Lackland Air Force Base in San Antonio, Texas, on December 17, 1978.

Shortly after we were married, a military doctor diagnosed Christine with having Asherman's syndrome, which is a rare condition that causes scarring on her uterus; more than 95 percent of her uterus was covered in scars. The condition can cause infertility, miscarriages, and severe pain. Christine underwent a procedure in July 1973 to remove the scarring, and she became pregnant with Trasa a little more than a year later.

We were so happy to have children of our own; they truly are God-given blessings. As it says in Psalm 127:3–5: *"Behold, children are a heritage from the Lord, the fruit of the womb a reward. Like arrows in the hand of a warrior are the children of one's youth. Blessed is the man who fills his quiver with them! He shall not be put to shame when he speaks with his enemies in the gate."*

In June 2014, after forty-three years of marriage to Christine, I wanted to do something really special for her. I realize the sacrifices she made during my military career, when she spent so many years away from her family and friends. After I left the army on January 31, 1993, Christine realized I wasn't happy living in Hollytree, Alabama, where we had decided to retire. She knew I wanted to be closer to my family so I could hunt and fish with Phil and his sons.

When Phil offered me a job at Duck Commander in 1999, Christine agreed to sell our house and move back to Louisiana. I thought she was seriously ill because she'd once told me she would never live in my home state again. When I was stationed at Fort Polk near Leesville, Louisiana, she hated living there. She didn't like the hot weather, high humidity, and mosquitoes—or Phil. But she knew that living closer to my family would make me happy, and she was willing to make that sacrifice for me.

---

Christine knew that living closer to my family would make me happy, and she was willing to make that sacrifice for me.

---

In hindsight, it was one of the best things we ever did. If I hadn't moved back to West Monroe, Louisiana, *Duck Dynasty* would have never happened—at least not for me. The show's producers and directors would have been forced to try to build a hit show around Willie and Jase, and I'm sure we can all guess how that would have turned out.

In the first *Duck Dynasty* episode of season four in 2013, Phil and his wife, Kay, renewed their wedding vows after forty-nine years of marriage. They'd been together since Kay was fourteen years old and were married by a justice of the peace, like Christine and me. So on their forty-ninth anniversary, their kids thought it would be great to give Kay the wedding she always dreamed of having.

My job on their wedding day was to keep them distracted, so everything could be set up for the surprise ceremony at their house. Well, I took them on a trip down memory lane. I took them back to their first house and to the tree on which they'd carved their initials together when they were teenagers. When we returned to their house, everybody was waiting for them. Their son Alan married them again, and I was Phil's best man. It was a beautiful ceremony.

As my forty-third wedding anniversary approached, I thought it would be nice to give Christine the wedding she'd never had. When you decide to reaffirm your wedding vows, you have to ask yourself this question: Would you do it all over again? Would you make the same decision and choose your honey as your life partner? There's no doubt in my mind that Christine was and always will be the one woman for me. Talk about a match made in heaven.

I wanted to make Christine's surprise wedding something really special. Her favorite musical group is the country duo Brooks & Dunn. Unfortunately, Kix Brooks and Ronnie

Dunn split up in 2010, so they couldn't sing at our wedding. I decided to do the next-best thing: I recorded a song with Brooks for a six-song EP that I gave Christine as a wedding present. I called the EP *Me and My Smokin' Hot Honey*. The EP contains a duet with Brooks and me singing, "Can't Take the Swamp Outta the Man." I flew to Nashville and sang my part at a recording studio. Brooks had already sung his lines during an earlier recording session, and producers worked their magic putting them together. The song is about how no amount of money could change my love for Christine. *There just ain't no 'mount of money that can change me and my smokin' hot honey*, Brooks sings.

The other songs on the EP include: "How Much I Love You," "Would You Marry Me Again," "His And Hers," "Faith, Hope And Love," and "If You Can't Dig That." Hey, there were a lot of people who helped me write and compose this love letter to my wife. Ashley Howard Nelson, Brandon Ray, Marcel Chagnon, Nathan Chapman, James Slater, Zach Harris, the Mauldin Brothers, and Jacob Lyda wrote the songs. My daughter-in-law, Marsha Robertson, sang one of the songs, and Jessica Andrews, Ally Moore, Macy Jae, and others also performed them. Ashley and Greg Droman produced the EP. Without their invaluable help, the EP would have never happened.

My wedding renewal day finally arrived on June 3, 2014, and we held the ceremony on the front lawn of my son's house in West Monroe. All of our family and friends were there, and it was a great big party. When Christine walked down the aisle, I surprised her by playing "Can't Take the

Swamp Outta the Man" for the first time. She couldn't believe Kix Brooks recorded a song for her! Brooks and Tricia
Yearwood were even kind enough to film personal messages
for her.

When it was time to exchange our vows a second time,
I pulled out a cigar band.

"You're not doing this again? Are you?" she asked me.

"Hey, Dad, I have your ring," said my son, Scott, who was
my best man.

After more than four decades of marriage, I finally slipped
a diamond ring onto Christine's finger. Hey, if it were up to
me, Christine would still be wearing a cigar band on her finger. After forty-three years of marriage, why would we want
to change our luck now?

But again, it wasn't about the ring or cigar band. It was
about the words we said to each other. Once again, we promised to "have and to hold, from this day forward, for better,
for worse, for richer, for poorer, in sickness or in health, to
love and to cherish till death do us part." My love for Christine is even stronger now than the day I met her.

Hey, people ask me all the time about the secrets to having a healthy, lasting marriage. They'll ask me, "How can
you be married to the same woman for so long? How do
you make it work?" The first thing you have to understand
is that marriage is a lifetime commitment, according to the
Bible. Too many people are getting married nowadays for the
wrong reasons. They figure if the marriage doesn't work out,
they can fix things in divorce court. That's not supposed to
be how it works.

The Bible says marriage is meant to be a special covenant between a man, a woman, and God. In Matthew 19:3–9, the Pharisees ask Jesus, *"Is it lawful for a man to divorce his wife for any and every reason?"* Jesus told them of God's purpose for marriage: *"Haven't you read," he replied, "that at the beginning the Creator 'made them male and female,' and said, 'For this reason a man will leave his father and mother and be united to his wife, and the two will become one flesh'? So they are no longer two, but one flesh. Therefore what God has joined together, let no one separate."*

Hey, marriage isn't easy. It's certainly no walk in the park. It is a long, winding road full of difficult choices, selflessness, and service to each other. At the same time, it's a journey full of blessings, joy, and hope. Marriage is about sacrifices—like the ones Christine made for me—and about constant devotion to each other. Look, no one is perfect. Everyone has bad days, yells at his or her spouse, and is selfish at times. Learn to say I'm sorry and apologize. Despite our imperfections, God created husband and wife to steer each other in His direction.

What's the best recipe for a strong marriage? The most important thing to do is to maintain your friendship with your honey. Look, you probably wouldn't have asked your husband or wife to marry you if he or she wasn't your best friend. Friendship is the foundation of every relationship. Christine was my best friend when I asked her to marry me, and she's still my best friend today. We love spending time together and experiencing things with each other.

Hey, a marriage won't last if you don't laugh together.

Make each other smile and have fun together. Find out what interests both of you and enjoy those things with each other. Make laughing, smiling, and crying tears of joy integral parts of your relationship.

---

**The most important thing to do is to maintain your friendship with your honey.**

---

You also need to make sure that you pay attention to your honey. Love means attention. Don't get so caught up in your career and hobbies that you neglect your spouse. One of the hardest things for young couples to do is juggle the day-to-day chaos of their lives. They spend so much time shuffling their kids through car pools, baseball practices, and dance recitals that they don't have time for each other.

Hey, don't wait until the next power failure to have a candlelight dinner with your honey. Take time to do sweet things for him or her. Buy her a dozen roses or write him a love letter. If your marriage is going to grow, you have to find time for each other.

The Good Lord knows I've enjoyed the first forty-five years of my marriage, and I'm looking forward to spending the rest of my life with Christine.

*Take delight in the Lord*

*and he will give you the desires of your heart.*

—PSALM 37:4 (NIV)

# CHAPTER 7

# BUCKET LIST

Do you remember that movie with Jack Nicholson and Morgan Freeman called *The Bucket List*? It was about two terminally ill men who shared a hospital room. One of them (Freeman) was a retired auto mechanic, while the other (Nicholson) was the billionaire owner of the hospital. They didn't have private rooms because Nicholson's character had instituted a cost-saving policy of no single rooms with no exceptions—even for him.

Even though the men were completely different in every way, they eventually figured out they shared one common characteristic—a lot of regret about how they had lived their lives. The auto mechanic started compiling a bucket list, which was a catalog of things he wanted to do before he died. He wanted to go skydiving, drive a race car, visit the Pyramids, see the Great Wall of China, and go on a safari in Africa. He was bitter that he didn't have the time or money to do any of them. Freeman's circumstances inspired the hospital owner, and he decided that they would do the things together before they died.

Hey, I was about to turn sixty years old when *The Bucket List* was released in 2007. After seeing the movie, Christine told me that I should come up with a bucket list of my own. "A bucket list?" I asked her. "Are you ready for me to kick the bucket?"

---

"A bucket list?" I asked Christine.
"Are you ready for me to kick the bucket?"

---

"No," she said. "Everybody should have a bucket list. It's everything you want to do before you die."

Well, I spent the next few days pondering what things should be on my bucket list. Hey, I know I have been very blessed. I have already experienced so much in my life that I never thought I would get a chance to do. The Good Lord has blessed my family and me with so many opportunities. For a poor country boy from Louisiana, I have already experienced so much. Among the things I've already done:

- I drove a monster truck.
- I wrote a *New York Times* No. 1 bestseller.
- I recorded a country-and-western album.
- I microwaved Ivory soap.
- I saw a black panther in the wild.
- I owned a racehorse.

- I wrote a children's book.
- I ate bacon and eggs for dinner.
- I sang at the Grand Ole Opry.
- I caught a world-record crappie.
- I wore a Scottish kilt.
- I made a bomb out of Mentos and Coca-Cola.
- I appeared as an extra in a Hollywood movie.
- I airboated across an alligator-infested swamp.
- I went bungee-jumping in Panama City Beach, Florida.
- I ran with scissors.

I think everybody should have a bucket list. For whatever reason, when you write your list on paper, it seems to motivate you to actually do the things you've listed. Look, the only people who fear death are those who don't have a relationship with the Lord and those who haven't truly lived yet. We can't be afraid to try new things and take chances. Hey, try a peanut butter and Tabasco sandwich every once in a while. You might be surprised by how good it tastes.

---

Hey, try a peanut butter and Tabasco
sandwich every once in a while. You might
be surprised by how good it tastes.

---

Make a list of the goals you want to achieve, the things you want to accomplish, dreams you want to fulfill, and the experiences you want to have before the Almighty decides your time on earth is up. Look at what you're doing with your life on a day-to-day basis and decide if life is passing you by. What have you done today? What are you doing tomorrow? What are you going to do next week? Do the things you're doing really mean much to you if you die next month?

Hey, don't get me wrong. Your life shouldn't be a race against time. Take time to stop and smell the roses and appreciate the people around you. Loving God, family, and friends is what's most important. But you should decide the things you want to do to live life to the fullest and what you want to achieve while you're on earth.

I had no idea there was still so much I wanted to do. Over the course of several days, I came up with a list of three hundred and thirteen things I want to do before I die. And then I started to whittle it down. Hey, there are still plenty of things I want to accomplish before I'm six feet under, including:

- Visit Stonehenge
- Learn to speak Swahili
- Wrestle on *Monday Night Raw*
- Throw tomatoes during La Tomatina
- Work as a Sherpa at Mount Kilimanjaro
- Fly in a hot-air balloon
- Compete in a triathlon
- Run with the bulls at Pamplona
- Be a member of the *Jeopardy!* studio audience

- Have six-pack abs
- Fly with the Blue Angels
- Make a hole-in-one in golf
- Create my own line of specialty pizzas called Uncle Si's Pizza Pies
- Win the World Series of Poker and have a poker tournament dedicated to me. I even want to serve as the tourney's TV commentator.
- Crowd-surf at an Eminem concert
- Sleep on a trampoline
- Go scuba diving and search for sunken treasure
- Solve Rubik's Cube in world record time
- Ride 2.7 seconds on a bull named Fu Man Chu
- Yell "Are you not entertained?" at the Roman Colosseum

Fortunately, I have already been able to do one of the things at the top of my list. Hey, driving a monster truck was El Numero Uno, Jack! There are several things I love about America: Uncle Sam, the Fourth of July, backyard barbecues, sweet tea, apple pie, fireworks, and monster trucks. Now, some of you might argue that monster trucks don't exactly belong on that list. But hey, it's my list.

For the life of me, I can't understand why monster trucks get such a bad rap from some people. Have you ever attended a monster truck event? If you've been to one, you know that it just might be the most exciting event in American sports. Hey, you can have the Super Bowl, Kentucky Derby, and World Series. I'll take Monster Jam any day of the week.

Where else can you find cars named the Big Kahuna, Bounty Hunter, El Toro Loco, Grave Digger, Ice Cream Man, Monster Mutt Rottweiler, Son-uva Digger, and Zombie Hunter flying thirty feet into the air and crushing old cars, vans, buses, motor homes, airplanes, and mobile homes? If that ain't America, I don't know what is. That's a fact, Jack!

Hey, the only thing I know that's more exciting than monster trucks is watching my nephew Jase trying to do Pilates! Let 'er rip, tater chip. Every time I've been to a monster truck event, I was on the edge of my seat for a couple of hours. In fact, the only thing that gets me more excited than monster trucks is walking into a new Bass Pro Shop.

I have always been fascinated by how the men and women behind the wheel of monster trucks can keep them from flipping over. I mean, it defies gravity! The trucks are about twelve feet tall and twelve feet wide. The trucks weigh a minimum of ten thousand pounds and have sixty-six-inch tires. How's that for being jacked up, Jack? Keeping that thing balanced on four wheels is like my nephew Willie trying to stay on his feet when he gets up from the dinner table on Thanksgiving Day. No matter how hard Willie tries, he's falling down like a rodeo clown!

Hey, driving monster trucks is a dangerous sport. The drivers are required to wear fire suits, safety harnesses, and helmets, as well as head and neck restraints. There are three "kill" switches to cut off the truck's engine and electricity if anything goes wrong. Believe me, when there's about 1,500 horsepower running on methanol under the hood, there's plenty that can go wrong.

I have always wanted to drive a monster truck. In fact, it was the main thing I wanted to do before the Good Lord decided it was my time to go. Thankfully, my dream came true in March 2014. I was sitting in my house in West Monroe, when the phone rang. Ryan Rice, who owns a monster truck named Incinerator, was on the other end.

*I'd only change one thing about monster trucks:*
*I'd add a cup holder for my cup of unsweet tea!*

"Hey, I'm down here at the Monroe Civic Center," Ryan said. "We're getting ready to do a monster truck show."

"Well, what do you want me to do?" I asked him.

"Do you want to drive one of these trucks?" he asked me.

Before Ryan could even hang up the phone, I was in my truck and driving to the arena. I met Ryan and his wife, Kari, and they introduced me to their crew chief. He spent an hour with me, showing me how to start the truck, kill the engine, and turn the wheel. Hey, I needed a ladder to climb into Incinerator. That's how big it is. I also didn't know monster-truck drivers sit in the middle of the cab so they can see out both sides. Talk about being in the captain's chair!

Ryan told me the plan was for me to kick off the show by driving Incinerator out to the track—and no further. I was only supposed to drive from one end of the arena to the other, past the stack of cars and trucks they were getting ready to crush, and stop and cut off the engine. Then I was supposed to climb out of the truck and wave to the crowd. Hey, simple enough.

It was pretty clear to me that Ryan didn't want a rookie driver like me wrecking his expensive truck. Hey, I couldn't blame him. It costs a lot of money to build a monster truck. The fiberglass body and chassis alone cost about $60,000. The custom-built, supercharged, big-block V8 engine costs another $50,000, and monster trucks go through about five of those engines every year. It isn't a cheap sport and it's not child's play, that's for sure. I promised Ryan I would follow his instructions.

Well, you know how I am about following directions.

While Ryan wanted me to do nothing more than to go for a Sunday drive, his crew chief had other ideas.

"Hey, what did the boss man tell you to do?" the crew chief asked me.

"He told me to drive by the line of old cars, climb out, take my helmet off, and wave to the fans," I told him.

"Hey, you don't need to do that," the crew chief said. "You need to jump something."

"Okay," I told him. "Tell me how to jump something."

The crew chief explained to me that I had to be sure I made a wide turn and that I lined up the truck's tires with the dirt ramp I was going to jump. Once I felt the tires go up the ramp, it was time to put the pedal to the metal. Then I was fixing to go airborne. He told me the most critical thing was to take my foot off the gas once the truck was in the air. When the truck hit the ground, I was supposed to turn the steering wheel and hit the gas again.

---

"Hey," the crew chief said.
"You need to jump something."

---

"This truck does awesome doughnuts," he said.

Well, I started the truck and pulled out onto the track. I gave a thumbs-up to Ryan and my buddy Phillip McMillan, whom Willie sent to the arena to make sure I didn't do anything crazy. Once I reached the other end of the arena,

I turned the truck around and headed for a dirt ramp—in a hurry! I wish you could have seen the look on Phillip's face. He looked like a deer in headlights. He knew we were fixing to have a hootenanny like he hadn't seen in his lifetime!

When Incinerator started climbing the dirt ramp, I floored the gas pedal. Of course, I remembered to take my foot off the gas once the truck was airborne. Unfortunately, the laws of physics wouldn't allow me to do it. When Incinerator was in the air, I was looking straight up at the ceiling of the Civic Center. When the truck started its descent, I was looking straight down at the dirt track. The only thing on my mind was to take my foot off the gas pedal, but I couldn't do it because all of my weight was on it!

Fortunately, Ryan had a remote kill switch for the engine. When he noticed I was in trouble, he cut off the truck's power. After a somewhat rocky landing, I climbed out of the truck, took off my helmet, and waved to the crowd. The place went nuts when the fans realized I was the one driving the truck. But when I reached Ryan and Phillip, they weren't smiling at all.

"What are you do doing?" Ryan asked me. "Are you nuts? Are you crazy? What were you thinking?"

"Hey, it had fifteen hundred horsepower," I said. "I had to see what it could do."

We all laughed about it. I thanked Ryan for letting me drive his truck, and he thanked me for putting on a good show for the fans.

"Hey, Robertson," he told me. "When *Duck Dynasty* goes

south, you've got a job driving my truck. That was the best stunt of the night."

I'm not going to lie: driving a monster truck was a lot harder than I thought it was going to be. Have you ever tried to keep a cup of tea from spilling while you're driving one of those monsters? Those trucks need cupholders, Jack!

Hey, I have been enamored with fast cars and have been sort of a gearhead since I was a little kid. I have always had a need for speed. There's nothing like the smell of burnt rubber on asphalt. It's kind of like the smell of napalm in the morning. If I could bottle that smell, I'd sell it as a fragrance. What can I say? I love fast cars, Jack!

Now, you might know that my family never had much in terms of material possessions when I was a kid. In fact, I didn't even own a car until after I joined the army. The first couple of cars I owned weren't very fast. I can remember going to an auto parts store to get a gas cap for my Plymouth. "Hey, I'd like a gas cap for my Plymouth," I told the man behind the counter. He looked at me for a couple of minutes and said, "Sounds like a fair trade."

When I was in high school, a buddy of mine had a 1966 Pontiac GTO. That car was beautiful, and boy, was it fast. It had a circular speedometer that went from zero to 120 miles per hour. One day after football practice, my buddy offered to give me a ride home. It was about a five-mile walk back to my house, so I accepted his offer.

When we reached the winding country road that went to my house, my buddy said, "Hey, let me show you what this thing will do." In an instant, we were going 100 miles per hour down the highway. I looked at the speedometer. The arrow reached 120 miles per hour and then it was back at zero. We must have been going 130 miles per hour! I don't know what was under the hood of his GTO, but it had serious firepower.

All of the sudden, my buddy slowed down his car. "Oh, I shouldn't be doing this," he said. "My right front tire is bald."

"Hey," I told him, "shut it down."

My friend pulled his car over to the side of the highway. I climbed out. "I'll walk the rest of the way," I said. What a knucklehead.

Riding in a NASCAR Sprint Cup stock car was also very high on my bucket list. It was right behind driving a monster truck. I was able to cross that achievement off my list in 2014, when Duck Commander became the title sponsor of the Duck Commander 500 at Texas Motor Speedway in Fort Worth. Justin Martin and I rode in the pace car with Sprint Cup driver Clint Bowyer at the start of the race. I was sitting in the passenger's seat, and Martin was sitting in the backseat.

Once we really started going, I looked out my window and saw about two inches between our car and the wall! Talk about cutting it close! Clint could tell I was getting a little nervous. "I can't go any faster," he said. "It will blow the lights off the top of the car. They don't like that." I looked at the speedometer. We were going 140 miles per hour! I served as grand marshal of the race and got to deliver the most famous words in auto racing: "Gentlemen, start your engines!"

I'll tell you one thing: Clint and the other Sprint Cup drivers were lucky I wasn't in the field that day. I would have put them in the wall or in the infield. After my spin in Incinerator, I am the demolition king.

Hey, I've been able to do a lot of things because of *Duck Dynasty*. I've been able to visit a lot of places that I wouldn't have gone to and meet a lot of people that I wouldn't have met. I count my blessings every day.

Not everything on your bucket list needs to cost money. The most important items on your list might include reconnecting with old friends, learning to play chess, telling your honey every day that you love him or her, giving a surprise to someone special, or performing a kind deed for someone without expecting something in return.

Hey, use your bucket list to make a difference in someone else's life. Volunteer for Habitat Humanity or another ministry. Mentor an at-risk child. Help feed and clothe the needy. Read the Bible every day or make a religious pilgrimage. Become more involved in your church. Make sure you're spending enough time with your spouse and children. Basically, try to become a better person.

---

Hey, use your bucket list to make a
difference in someone else's life.

---

The thing I really liked about *The Bucket List* movie is that it was a story about redemption. While the two men were traveling around the world on a private jet, they realized how much their lives were changed by the relationship that developed between them along the journey. Hey, folks, the bottom line is love. We are redeemed by our love for God and each other. In the end, seeing the Great Wall of China and the Pyramids wasn't what was important. It was the fact that the two guys became great friends and experienced their adventures together.

Hey, believe me, time does fly by when you get older. The days, weeks, months, and years seem so much shorter. In Psalm 39: 4–5, David asked God to remind him how brief his time would be on earth: *"Show me, Lord, my life's end and the number of my days; let me know how fleeting my life is. You have made my days a mere handbreadth; the span of my years is as nothing before you. Everyone is but a breath, even those who seem secure."*

Our time on earth is short, especially in the grand scheme of eternity. Put together a bucket list. Decide what's truly important to you, what you want to accomplish, what changes you want to make in your life, and what you can do to help others. Quit putting off things you want to achieve, and don't be afraid to take chances. Remember that through Jesus Christ we have the power to tackle anything. As it says in Philippians 4:13: *"I can do all this through him who gives me strength."*

Get your relationship with the Almighty in order, and love your family and friends like you've never loved them before. Live your life for God. Ask Him what He wants you to do and not what you want to do. Do what Tim McGraw says to do in his "Live Like You Were Dying" song: love deeper, speak sweeter, and give forgiveness you've been denying. Hey, live like you were dying. Before you and I know it, there won't be time left to do it.

# HALLU-SI-NATIONS

## Golf

Hey, I've never quite figured out why my nephews enjoy playing golf so much. They play nearly every weekend with their friends, and when they're done, they're in such a bad mood. At one time, my nephew Willie actually wanted to be a professional golfer. Hey, the first time I saw Willie break 70, he was so excited he forgot to play the last nine holes!

*Playing golf with my nephews Jase, Alan, Jep, and Willie is one of my favorite things to do, especially when it involves beating Jase! We played together in Scotland in 2014.*

Golf is such a strange game. You hit the ball down to make it go up. You swing left and the ball goes right. You swing right and it goes left. The lowest score wins, and, on top of that, the winner has to buy drinks for the losers! You figure it out! Well, I caught the golf bug a couple of years ago. I took lessons from Matt Owens at the Trenton Street Golf Course in West Monroe, Louisiana. After a couple of hours, I'd mastered the game. Now, I like to call myself an amateur player but a professional instructor. I mostly play in the low eighties. Hey, if it's hotter than that, you won't find me on a golf course.

I've learned that golfers are a very curious bunch. They put way too much pressure on themselves when they're playing, and they overanalyze everything. Hey, look, golf is a very simple game. The only objective is to get the little white ball into the hole. It's not that hard, okay? People make the game way too complicated.

There are four basic simple steps to becoming a good golfer: stance, swing, mastering your long putts, and not overdoing it. When it comes to your stance, hey, set your feet up so you can hit the ball. Mastering your swing is just as easy. If you want to hit the ball a long way, swing harder. If you want to hit a short shot, swing softer. You get the idea.

Hey, long putts might be the most important part of golf. If you can make long putts, you won't have to worry about the short ones. It all goes back to my philosophy of not overdoing it. Don't think too much when you're playing golf. Clear your head and have fun. It's much easier to play when you're not thinking about a million things.

Now, the most important rule in golf—and the Good Lord knows there are hundreds of them—is that you have to look the part. You can't go out to the golf course dressed like a buffoon. You can have a horrible game, but as long as you do it with class, nobody is going to give a flip. Hey, look like the guys you see playing on TV.

---

Now, the most important rule in golf
is that you have to look the part.

---

Another important thing I've learned about golf is that it's a lot like fishing. You need a lot of patience, and there's a lot of standing around—especially when you're playing with my nephew Jase. Hey, Jase hits the woods great. He only has problems getting out of them! The biggest difference between golf and fishing: you don't have to have visual evidence to tell a great story about your golf feats.

A couple of years ago, I played golf with my friend Phillip McMillan and two others at the Dancing Rabbit Golf Club in Philadelphia, Mississippi. It's a beautiful course and was a lot of fun to play. We were playing a scramble, which meant that Phillip and I could use each other's shots to compile the lowest score on each hole.

Going into the eighteenth hole, our match was dead even. Phillip hit his tee shot into the woods. It was my turn to hit my tee shot.

"Hey, please hit it down the middle," Phillip said. "Just swing nice and easy and pop the ball down the middle. Make sure we have a good second shot."

"Nah," I said. "No can do, partner. I'm going for it. I'm going to let 'er rip."

I pulled back my driver and swung with all of the strength in my body. Much to Phillip's surprise, my drive was long, high, and straight down the middle!

"Hey, if that ball clears the bunker, we're going to be in great shape," Phillip said.

We jumped in our golf cart and drove down the fairway. We looked in the bunker and didn't see my ball. In fact, we didn't see it anywhere.

"Hey, if y'all are looking for Si's ball, it's way up there," one of our opponents said.

We looked down the fairway and saw a little white speck in the distance. "Hey, stop everything, boys," I said. "Jase isn't going to believe this."

I asked Phillip and the other players to pose for a photograph with me right there in the middle of the fairway. Each of us held up three fingers, signaling my 300-yard drive. We ended up with a birdie on the last hole and won the match.

When we went home the next day, I showed Jase the picture of my 300-yard drive.

"That doesn't prove anything," he said. "You were probably lying there after three shots."

Just like with the black panther, even photo evidence couldn't convince Jase that it was true. This time, though, I had three other witnesses to prove that it was.

*Make a joyful noise unto the Lord. . . .*

*Serve the Lord with gladness:*

*come before his presence with singing.*

—Psalm 100:1–2 (KJV)

# CHAPTER 8

# GUITAR HERO

I've always liked to sing, and fortunately the Good Lord blessed me with a loud, booming voice. More than anything, I like to make loud, joyful noises. Hey, that's what the Good Book tells us to do! I like to sing just about everywhere: in the shower, in my truck, in the duck blind, on the front porch, and in the bed. I especially like singing at church. Singing at church always fills me with peace and si-renity. There's just something about praising the One who made us that calms our souls.

Now, I've never claimed to be a great singer, but I like to think I'm pretty entertaining. Like everything else I do in life, I try to have fun while I'm singing. I know my voice is far from polished. It's more of a work in progress. In fact, my vocal range is kind of like a mutt—it's a mix of bass, baritone, tenor, and alto! When I sing inside the house, Christine tells me to be quiet because our windows aren't insured.

Over the years, I've figured out that singing is kind of like locking myself out of my truck—I can never find the right key! In fact, there have been more than a few times in church when the sweet little lady sitting in front of me has suddenly stood up, stuck her fingers in her ears, and walked out of Sunday morning service. Hey, I know my voice isn't for everyone! It's kind of like unsweetened tea—it's an acquired taste.

Though I started singing when I was very young, I never learned how to play the guitar, which is something I've always wanted to do. I'm a big fan of legendary guitarists like Jimi Hendrix, Eric Clapton, Jimmy Page, Eddie Van Halen, B. B. King, and Stevie Ray Vaughan. When I was in the army and stationed in Vietnam, I liked to listen to the Rolling Stones and Led Zeppelin. That's the kind of music we listened to during the 1960s. Later, rock bands like AC/DC and Van Halen were popular. I'll tell you one thing: I'm far more interested in a Stairway to Heaven than a Highway to Hell. You know what I'm saying, Jack?

---

**I'm far more interested in a Stairway
to Heaven than a Highway to Hell.**

---

Anyway, I've always wanted to learn how to play guitar, but never had the money to buy one or the time or patience to learn how to play it. Not too long ago, I was invited to attend a charity concert in Shreveport, Louisiana. Chris Cagle, a country singer from DeRidder, Louisiana, was the main attraction. Chris grew up in Texas and moved to Nashville,

*Isn't it funny that we don't discover many of our talents until much later in life? I never knew I could sing like Pavarotti and play guitar like Jimi Hendrix until I tried.*

where he paid his dues to become a big-time musician. He waited tables and even worked as a nanny while mastering his art. Eventually, he signed a recording deal with Virgin Records and released five albums. Some of his hit songs include "I Breathe In, I Breathe Out" and "Laredo." My personal favorite might be "Wal-Mart Parking Lot." Hey, who doesn't like cruising in a Walmart parking lot?

Before the charity concert, I met Chris and he invited me to come on stage and sing with him. He told me he was going to hand me a guitar when I was out there.

"What are you going to do with it?" he asked me.

"I'm going to let it rip," I said.

"I'll give you a guitar and it won't be hooked up to an amp," Chris said. "We call it air guitar. Just follow my lead."

When I walked out onto the stage, the crowd went nuts. One of the roadies handed me a guitar, and I watched Chris and his bass player and followed their lead. I was going crazy with the guitar, and the fans actually believed I was playing it! One of the guys backstage told my buddy Phillip McMillan: "Man, I didn't know Si could play a guitar like that." Phillip said: "Oh, he can skin it." I played a couple of songs with Chris and his band, and then the crowd wanted an encore. I went back onstage and played three more songs with them.

Needless to say, the excitement and rush from that night had me hooked. I'd never felt so much adrenaline. I had to learn how to play guitar! I told Phillip to find me a guitar instructor as soon as possible. Once I started my lessons, it didn't take me long to figure out that plucking duck feathers is a lot easier than plucking guitar strings. In many ways, marriage is a lot like playing guitar. It looks pretty easy until you actually try it! No matter how hard I tried, I couldn't figure out how to play a guitar. I always seemed to be out of tune and learning the chords was nearly impossible for me. Do you know the difference between a John Deere tractor and an electric guitar? You can actually tune the tractor, Jack!

Plucking duck feathers is a lot easier
than plucking guitar strings.

After a few weeks, I was pretty discouraged. My teachers
were even more frustrated. Two of them actually walked
out on me and said I was a lost cause. I have to admit: I was
beginning to think the music industry and I might not be a
good match. I needed a duet-yourself kit, if you know what
I mean. I knew that with my voice, I could become a pretty
good country-and-western singer, if I could only learn how
to play a guitar.

Fortunately, the Good Lord sent me an angel. Travis
Perry was a real estate agent in Dothan, Alabama, until the
housing market crashed. Then he opened a music store and
started teaching guitar lessons. In 2010, Travis invented a
device called the ChordBuddy to help his daughter learn
how to play guitar. You might have seen him on ABC's
*Shark Tank* not too long ago. The ChordBuddy is a magical,
color-coded device that attaches to the neck of a guitar. Travis says the ChordBuddy has a 90 percent success rate and al-
lows students to learn how to play guitar in only a few weeks.

Travis came to my house and worked with me for a few
days. He showed me how the ChordBuddy worked, and
I was strumming six strings before too long. Hey, I still have
a long way to go. I'm not actually making music yet, but I'm
making plenty of progress. My momma and daddy didn't

raise a quitter, Jack! Travis asked me what kind of music I wanted to play. I told him I preferred country and western, but I thought I might broaden my horizons once I mastered the guitar. I could even see myself singing a cappella or opera one day.

Travis and I became good friends, and he invited me to Dothan to perform with his bluegrass band last summer. I didn't play the guitar with them, but I sang George Jones's hit song "He Stopped Loving Her Today," and Willie Nelson's "Seven Spanish Angels." Later that night, Travis asked me if I wanted to go see one of his buddy's bands play at a dance hall. His friend Jeff Gordon had a very good singing voice and was a heck of an entertainer. As I watched him, I thought to myself, *I can do this.* After a few songs, Travis asked me if I wanted to perform with Jeff. "I think he knows George Jones," Travis said.

As soon as I heard "George Jones," I jumped up on stage with Jeff. I sang a few songs with his band, and the crowd went crazy. Jeff's band started playing Don Williams's hit song "Tulsa Time," and he asked me if I knew the lyrics. "No," I told him, "but start singing it, and I'll catch up with you."

"You're crazy, Robertson," Jeff told me. "You act like you've been up on stage forever."

One day, I might hit the road with Travis and his band. We already have a name for our band—Si Robertson and the Si-clones. That has a nice ring to it, don't you think?

A few months after I met Travis, Avery Michaels, a

country-and-western singer from Jena, Louisiana, did a show at my nephew Willie Robertson's restaurant—Willie's Duck Diner in West Monroe. I got to perform with Avery, and we had a real connection on stage. Avery's actual name is Avery Michael Belgard, and his father, Harvey Belgard, is also a very accomplished musician. His dad turned down a recording contract in 1953 because he didn't want to move his family to Nashville. He wanted to stay in a small town where he could raise his five children in a church. I've been to Avery's father's house and picked on the porch with him. His father is so talented that he can make the sounds of a harmonica—without actually having the musical instrument in his hands! I'm telling you, when the Good Lord designed the human body, he spent extra time on the vocal cords. It's absolutely amazing what a voice can do.

Avery and I have played together a few times over the past couple of years. We performed at the Duck Commander warehouse on the Fourth of July in 2015. When I learn how to play the guitar well, I might even go on the road with him.

In only a short time, I've made a lot of great memories in music and played with many talented musicians. I was fortunate enough to sing "Wagon Wheel" with Darius Rucker and my daughter-in-law, Marsha, who is married to my son, Scott. I'd previously appeared in one of Darius's music videos, and he's such a great guy. I also played with the Mauldin Brothers outside Rippy's in Nashville.

In 2013, my family released a Christmas CD called *Duck the Halls: A Robertson Family Christmas*. I sang "Hairy Christmas" with Luke Bryan, my brother Phil, and my nephews, Jase and Jep. I also sang a few others songs, such as "You're a Mean One, Mr. Grinch" and "The Night Before Christmas." It was a lot of fun and the CD received mostly positive reviews. I even recorded a song with Kix Brooks from Brooks & Dunn on the CD.

Now, the highlight of my music career occurred on November 14, 2015. On that night, I had the unbelievable honor of performing with Billy Dean and Billy Ray Cyrus at the Grand Ole Opry in Nashville. When I walked on stage with Billy Dean, he could sense that I was very nervous playing on country music's most famous stage.

"Hey, brother, I'm right there with you," Billy told me. "It happens to me every time I sing here. It's kind of like a dream for people in the business. It's when they can say, 'I've made it.'"

I couldn't believe I was standing where George Jones once stood and sang. Not only him—all the legendary singers in country-and-western music have performed there, and I now had the same honor. I looked down at the eight-foot wooden circle on the stage that came from Ryman Auditorium, the Grand Ole Opry's home from 1943 to 1974, and took a deep breath. I knew there were men and women in country music who would cut off their arms to sing at the Grand Ole Opry. I knew how truly lucky I was. Marsha and I sang "I Miss Billy the Kid" with Billy Dean, and "Some Gave All" with Billy Ray Cyrus. It was a night Marsha and I will never forget.

One thing I've learned about the music industry is that it's a tough business to make it big in. I'm fortunate in that I get to sing and play guitar without needing the money to pay my bills. I'd hate to have to do it to make a living. Everything has to line up perfectly for someone to hit it big in Nashville.

I couldn't believe I was standing where
George Jones once stood and sang.

I enjoy singing and playing guitar and it's a good way for me to unwind. I'm confident music is going to be my future. When *Duck Dynasty* goes down the drain, Silas Merritt Robertson is going to hit the road. I'm going on tour, and I'll be back at the Grand Ole Opry one day.

*A friend loves at all times,*

*and a brother is born for a time of adversity.*

—PROVERBS 17:17 (NIV)

# CHAPTER 9

# HOUSE OF CARDS

I can't tell you how many times people have approached me at gas stations, restaurants, and other public places in West Monroe, Louisiana, to tell me that I play poker with their father, brother, son, or husband.

The conversation undoubtedly starts like this: "Hey, Si, you play poker with my dad. His name is Bob so-and-so."

"Nope, I've never heard of him," I'll say.

"Oh, he says he plays with you," the lady will say. "He's a big tall guy with red hair and a goatee. He works down at the bank."

"Oh," I'll say. "You're talking about Chicken."

As long as we're not filming *Duck Dynasty* or I'm not out of town hunting or traveling to some event, I usually play poker with my buddies about once a week. It's what we like to do for fun, and I love spending a few hours with some of my closest friends. It's a great time for fellowship and entertainment.

*I love playing poker with my closest friends on Friday nights,
guys like Bull, Nerds, Chicken, Fox, and Prime Time.*

I still don't know most of their real names, even after
playing poker with those guys all of these years. To me, their
names are Bull, Nerds, Chicken, Fox, Prime Time, The

Counselor, Pim, and Curly Don. I'm sure their families call them by their actual names, but I wouldn't know what they are. All of those guys are great people. We don't get mad at each other while we're playing poker, even if one of us is losing. I know that if any one of us were in a bind, the rest of us would give him the shirts off our backs.

I grew up playing card games, board games, and dominoes with my brothers, sisters, and parents. Now that I'm older, I still play those games with my kids, grandkids, nephews, and nieces. The Robertsons have always been a competitive family, and we like to play each other in any game that involves chance. I'll play about any card game: solitaire, blackjack, hearts, gin rummy, go fish, war, crazy eights, spit, spades, Uno, old maid, and even euchre.

---

Robertsons have always been a competitive
family, and we like to play each other in
any game that involves chance.

---

But Texas Hold'em poker is absolutely my favorite card game to play. If you really want to learn about the Texas Hold'em game, there are plenty of books about it. ESPN and other TV networks broadcast poker tournaments all the time, and I like to watch them to see how the pros play. But if you really want to learn to play, you need to ask yourself this very important question: What does the *Book of Si* say about playing Texas Hold'em, Jack?

Here's the deal, right out of the gate: If you want to play Texas Hold'em for entertainment purposes only, then what I'm about to tell you probably isn't good advice. You can play the game for fun and still win every once in a while. But if you're going to play the game, I think you should at least set your mind to trying to win. You don't even have to play for money, but when I sit down at a table, I'm in it to win it, Jack!

Now, my number-one rule in poker is the same number-one rule in life: Keep your life in order. If your relationships are good with the Almighty, your wife or girlfriend, and your family and friends, then it's probably okay to have some extracurricular activities like playing poker. If things aren't good at home, however, you need to spend your time making them right. That's the most important rule in poker.

Before you sit down at a table, determine what your goals and objectives are going to be that night. If you play for money and you need to pay bills and support your family with your extra money, then choose your family and don't play poker. If you don't have a lot of disposable income, hey, only play for fun or low stakes—maybe the price of movie tickets for you and your honey, and also a bucket of popcorn with butter and a candy bar if you need it. If your truck payment or rent is riding on your poker hand, you shouldn't be sitting at a table. Do not shirk your responsibility as the breadwinner in your family. Make sure you have your life right and your ducks in a row before you pick up a hobby like playing poker.

Rule number two: Surround yourself with card players similar to yourself. You don't want to be sitting at a card table with a bunch of cheaters and crooks. Hey, do you know why poker isn't allowed in Africa? Because of all the cheetahs, Jack! Too many people are trying to make a living at a game. It's a *game,* folks. Only play with other people who have the same mind-set as you. Don't get mixed up playing cards with people who aren't there to have fun and enjoy each other's company. Try to play poker with people you enjoy being around. It's a good rule of Si.

---

If your truck payment or rent is riding on your poker hand, you shouldn't be sitting at a table.

---

Like I said earlier, I play cards for fellowship and entertainment. When I first started playing cards with my boys, I told them, "I'm only in this for the fun and fellowship. When that ends, I'm done." I love to laugh and clown around. I'm the joker of poker. The poker table is a great place to have fun with your family and good friends. I have the pleasure of playing cards with my closest friends and family members, and that's a good thing. I've also had the pleasure of playing with some great *Duck Dynasty* fans and army buddies. We're only there to have a good time.

Now that we're all on the same page, let's get started on what I like to call the basics of Texas Hold'em.

*Strategy:* There are several things you have to consider before the game even begins: your strategy, dos and don'ts, knowing your opponent, seating position, dealing with maniacs, loosening up tight players, setting goals, and, most important, making sure you have enough unsweetened tea on hand in case the game turns into a marathon.

Ask yourself this: What's my strategy going to be? We don't walk out to the duck blind and just start shooting (well, unless my nephew Willie is with us). There is a lot of preparation that takes place in advance. The duck hole needs to be scouted, blinds have to be built and covered with brush, decoys have to be placed on the water just right, weather forecasts and wind direction have to be analyzed, weapons have to be cleaned and readied, food has to be made, and we have to figure out how we're going to get to the blind and leave safely. Hey, it takes a lot of work to go duck hunting with the Robertsons.

It's the same way with playing Texas Hold'em. You have to know what your plan is going to be going in. If you're playing to enjoy yourself and just pass the time, then stick to your plan. Play as long as you want and then call it a night. If you're playing to win, you need to remember these critical points. The best coaches in football and other sports often win before the games are even played. They do their homework, scout their opponents, and develop their strategies before the ball is even kicked off. It's the same way in poker.

Another thing to remember is that you can't focus on only one player. If you're not paying attention to everyone at the table, you might get side swiped by friendly fire. If you've ever been in a duck blind with Willie, you'd know exactly what I'm talking about. You have to have your head on a swivel when you're shooting ducks with Willie, Jack! You never know when a few pellets might buzz your ears.

Pay attention to everyone at the table and know exactly how many chips they have in their stacks. Don't go on the tilt and lose your strategy. I've watched plenty of good players play tight all night, but then lose their entire stack in only a couple of hands because they went on the tilt. You have to have a little common sense and play with self-control. Whatever you do, don't get involved in too many pots and, most important, learn to fold. This is a difficulty strategy to learn—even for me. Remember that the most underrated play is folding.

*Scouting:* I know the guys I play poker with: Bull, Fox, Chicken, Nerds, McMillan, Jase, Willie, Jep, Martin, Terry Mac, Frank, The Counselor, John Carter, and many more. When I say I know these guys, I mean I *know* them. I know how they like to play. I know who is a poker bully and who is full of bull. I know their tendencies and patterns. I know some of them are capable of playing good poker, while some of them don't know the difference between a good hand and a bad hand. Some of them even like to try to win with tricks and nonsense.

I do know this: What is known is manageable. Once I know a person's tendencies and strategy, I can make my own deductions and conclusions. You might be surprised to know that I'm not exactly playing the person but their hand. It usually works out pretty well for me. When I decide that

I have a read on an opponent's hand, I'll go with the read. If you can't stick with your initial read and listen to what your gut is saying, then you don't need to play. It's a tough strategy to live by, but it's worthwhile.

*Seating position:* When we go duck hunting, it seems like my brother Phil and Jase always have the best seating positions in the blind, which are on opposite ends. Nobody shoots a duck until one of them says, "Cut 'em." Since they're going to see the ducks first and decide when everyone else gets to shoot, they usually have the best shots at the ducks. Everyone else gets the leftovers. It's like when we were kids sitting at the dinner table. The adults ate first and then the kids ate whatever was left, which usually wasn't much.

In Texas Hold'em poker, you pretty much get to decide where you sit, unless you decide ahead of time that everyone is going to draw for a seat. The most important thing you want to remember about seating is that you never want to sit next to a maniac. A maniac is someone who doesn't have a strategy. If you have a maniac in your poker game, make sure you sit to his left. You don't want to sit to his right because then he'll be making decisions on his hand after you act. It can mess up the entire game.

The most important thing you want to remember about seating is that you never want to sit next to a maniac.

Over the years, I've learned that the only way to beat a maniac is to slow-play my big hands and then let him bluff his chips away. Remember: the trapper thinks two steps ahead of his victim. It's like a big chip explosion when it happens. Boom! There goes his stack of chips, exploding like my old gray truck and landing in my stack. You can't buy that kind of entertainment anywhere. That's what I'm talking about, Jack!

Now, on the other hand, when you have a tight player that you're trying to beat, you have to be a little tricky. You have to show a lot of bluffs and overbet the pot at times, especially when you have the solid gold nuts in your hand. Sometimes, you'll get caught and they'll sniff you out, which Jase is pretty adept at doing with me. I'm telling you: that boy could smell a skunk from nine miles away! He always seems to know when I have him beat. Tight players are sometimes difficult to beat. Sometimes, I can persuade a tight player to call his hand by acting weak. I'm not an actor but I can tell a good story. That's another important lesson: Tell your story with enthusiasm! Don't forget that, boys.

*Holding it together:* When I watch professional poker players on TV, the good ones seem to play with one common attribute—consistency. Poker is the only sport in which professionals and amateurs often play together, and in most cases the pros might not be overwhelming favorites. In the end, it always depends on the cards. On some nights, you'll catch good hands; some nights you won't. The most important thing is to remember to hold it together. Play with patience and have fun. Try to enjoy the game, whether you're winning or not.

*Taunting:* Just like when I'm playing rook, chess, dominoes, spades, or Scrabble, playing poker with me can be brutal. If you're thin-skinned and get your feelings hurt easily, like Willie, poker might not be the right game for you. Warning: turn back now! I will still respect you, but I don't want to see you cry. I like to talk it up a little bit every now and then to make my opponents think there's more at stake than there actually is.

---

If you're thin-skinned and get your feelings hurt easily, like Willie, poker might not be the right game for you.

---

I learned this skill at a young age. In our regular card games when I was a kid, we liked to say that our game was the "shark tank." The brim bed and the kiddie games were being played down the street. It was really only plain fun, but when the Robertson family plays cards or dominoes, it's like we're in it for blood. It isn't for the faint of heart, that's for sure.

Before I started playing with my buddies, the games usually involved only family members and our closest friends. We love to beat each other and then rub it in. If Jase plays a bad hand, I'm going to tell him about it. I'm not worried about hurting his feelings. If Jase screws up a hand, I'm going to go step by step on how he messed up, and everyone else at the table is going to dissect his errors too. It's the way we play.

Hey, I've had Willie so mad at the table that he has actually left the game crying. Well, at least that's how I remember it. He would probably say different. Do you know the difference between Willie and an old hound dog? After a while, the dog eventually quits whining.

Jase is as slippery as a fish in shallow water when he's playing poker. He seems to win a lot because he plays super tight. Jase is so tight with his money that he'll only invite me to dinner when he has a two-for-one coupon. When it's time to pay, he makes me pay the entire bill! Phil's youngest son, Jep, hates to lose, especially to his older brothers, Jase and Willie. Jep plays pretty good poker. Jep's wife, Jessica, and Korie also play good poker.

Justin Martin, who works with me in the reed room at Duck Commander, plays poker with us every once in a while. He likes to call our game "plinko," whatever that means. One night, Martin wanted to quit because he was taking so many bad beats. Willie told him to buy back into the game or he was going to dock his pay. Now, that's funny!

A few members of the Robertson clan are good poker players, but I think I have the edge on all of them. It could be that icy stare that you might have heard about. Or it could be that I don't believe them most of the time, especially Willie, who is the classic bluffer. Willie is not going to bluff me. He knows it and I know it. One day, Willie is going to learn that I'm a mind reader when it comes to his brain. Fortunately, there isn't much inside his head to figure out!

*Bluffing:* The best qualifying hands in Texas Hold'em are obviously pocket aces, kings, queens, jacks, and so forth. Other hands to consider are ace-king, ace-queen, ace-jack, especially if they're of the same suit. Now, some people are going to tell you that you should only play these premium hands before the flop. I'm here to tell you that you need more than that in your arsenal. You have to be willing to play less than premium hands and learn to run "without the ball."

---

One day, Willie is going to learn that I'm a
mind reader when it comes to his brain.

---

Believe it or not, there's a science behind it. The Good Lord blessed me with the art of storytelling and it certainly comes in handy at a poker table. The correct terminology is bluffing. If you tell a good story, there's a good chance others will believe it, regardless of how far-fetched it might seem. Learn to tell a believable story when you're bluffing. You have to be willing to push your chips with a real hand or a bluffing hand with equal enthusiasm.

*Ride the wave:* For some players, being lucky is an art. For whatever reason, I've always been lucky. I'm talking 'bout, hey, a penny on the head, inside a horseshoe, on top of a four-leaf clover, and rolled up with a leprechaun kind of lucky. Four-leafed clovers don't find themselves. You gotta get down and look for 'em.

There have been many times when I've busted an entire

table with nothing in my hand. It isn't necessarily because I'm such a good player. I have the uncanny ability to recognize when things are going my way. I like to ride the wave when it's rolling. My friends call it the Si-Cycle, and it's a ride that demands respect. When I'm on a heater, it seems like I can catch the exact cards needed to win. While it might sound a little absurd, it's actually reality. My advice to you is to ride the wave when it's rolling!

*Profiling:* Pay close attention to this: you have to decide what kind of player you want to be. I'm the type of person who plays the hand. You might be the type of person who plays the odds and pulls out a slide ruler every time someone checks or raises you. That's fine. I'm only saying that I'm more of a "feel" kind of player. I can play with a person and figure out his patterns pretty easily. Some people have a tendency to do the same things over and over, depending on whether they have a good hand or a bad one. In most cases, they probably don't even know they're doing it.

---

If you tell a good story, there's a good chance others will believe it.

---

One of the guys who plays poker with us pretty regularly is a man we call Nerds. Now, Nerds is a pretty good player. But he used to have what's called a "tell." He unknowingly rubbed his eyes when he had a big hand. Every time Nerds got into a big pot and rubbed his eyes, I immediately folded.

Hey, the other guys at the table never noticed him rubbing his eyes, so they would play with him and call him down to the river. Unknowingly, they'd lose a stack of chips every time against his big hand.

It might be because I grew up in the woods, but I pay close attention to my surroundings and environment. In the game of poker, you have to pay close attention to your opponents. You have to notice what they're doing and look for tells. By the way, after Nerds noticed me folding on every one of his big hands, he stopped rubbing his eyes. But what he doesn't know is that he started rubbing his ears. I'm certainly not going to tell him!

*The Big Coon hunts late:* Over the years, I've acquired quite a few nicknames at the poker table: The Si-Cycle, Any Two Magoo, Ain't Enough Nut, One-Pot Wonder, The Go-Bust Specialist, See-Saw Si, The Calling Station, The Magician (with the vanishing stack), and The Donkey Whisperer, among others.

What you need to know more than anything else is that I'm always in control. I'm a lot like the legendary poker player Gus Hansen—you never know what you're going to get when I sit down at the table. I like it that way. Changing my game and strategy is my secret to success. Just when my opponents think they have me pegged—boom!—I change it up and bust the table. I don't mind the funny names they call me, as long as they keep handing over their chips. You can't defend something you don't understand and can't predict. I'm like a flash of lightning. You never really know where it came from until it's too late.

I don't mind the funny names they call me, as
long as they keep handing over their chips.

One thing my opponents have learned over the years: the
later the night gets in a poker game, the more lethal I become. That's when I start plotting my attack without mercy.
Once that happens, it's time for the big coon to eat. Booya!

# HALLU-SI-NATIONS
## Birthday Parties

Hey, for the life of me, I can't figure out why April 27 isn't a national holiday. There were so many great people born on that date.

Ulysses S. Grant, eighteenth US President, was born on April 27, 1822. *American Top 40* host Casey Kasem was born on that date in 1932, and legendary bowler Earl Anthony came into the world on the same date six years later. KISS lead guitarist Ace Frehley was born on April 27, 1951, and basketball legend George "The Iceman" Gervin arrived exactly one year later.

Of course, Silas Merritt Robertson was born in Vivian, Louisiana, on April 27, 1948. Hey, I share the exact same birthday as B-52s lead singer, Kate Pierson. Who doesn't love their songs "Love Shack" and "Rock Lobster"? Plus, they make a great vitamin, Jack!

Hey, I love celebrating my birthday. I'm sixty-eight years old, and the Good Lord willing, I'm going to have quite a few more birthdays on this side of heaven. Fortunately, I have a loving family and very good friends who enjoy celebrating my birthdays with me.

When I turned sixty-five years old, in 2013, the guys I play poker with every week wanted to throw me a special surprise party with a big poker game. To pull it off, though, they had to play a really funny practical joke on me.

My best friend, Phillip McMillan, was the main organizer. He knows I love everything about Native American culture.

I grew up playing cowboys and Indians, and I still collect arrowheads and other artifacts. I'll buy Native American jewelry, beads, moccasins, clothes, tanned hides, baskets, and anything else I can get my hands on.

Well, Phillip and my buddies decided to rent out a store in a strip mall in West Monroe, Louisiana. About a week before my birthday, they printed advertising signs for a Cherokee Nation auction at the store. One of my friends, Marshall William Guyton, personally delivered me a flyer for the auction. I found another one on the windshield of my truck later in the week.

That Friday night, Phillip picked me up to take me to our weekly poker game at our friend Jeff Williams's house (we call him Nurse). During the drive there, Phillip put his phone on speaker and called Nurse's house.

"Hey, guys, I have some bad news," Nurse said. "Unfortunately, we can't play poker tonight. Something came up and the game has been canceled. I've already called the other guys."

Phillip hung up the phone. I shook my head and said, "Pitiful. I was really looking forward to playing poker on my birthday. Are you sure we can't get a game up?"

"No, he's already called everybody else and canceled the game," Phillip said.

"Well, just take me home then," I said.

"Wait, did you hear about this Native American auction?" Phillip asked. "There's nothing else to do. We might as well go by there. You might even be able to find you an authentic bow and arrow."

"Oh, yeah," I said. "I got one of their flyers. Let's go see what it's all about."

Phillip pulled his truck into the strip mall. From the parking lot, I heard drums beating and Native Americans chanting. Honestly, it sounded kind of spooky.

"Hold up," I said. "I don't know about this."

"Nah, let's go in and see what's happening," Phillip said. "If we don't like it, we can leave."

We walked into the dark store and could only see silhouettes in the back of the room. There was only a dim light in the front. I saw a handful of men chanting and dancing in a circle. They were wearing Native American headdresses and were carrying tomahawks over their heads.

"Nope, we're out of here," I said.

"Let's just take a seat in the back and see what happens," Phillip said.

Hey, I'll admit I was pretty nervous. I was holding on to my iced-tea glass extra tight. After a couple of minutes, the lights suddenly came on. The Native Americans looked at me and screamed, "Happy birthday!"

---

Hey, I'll admit I was pretty nervous. I was
holding on to my iced-tea glass extra tight.

---

I burst out laughing. I couldn't believe my buddies had tricked me so easily.

"Boys, I thought I had run across some kind of cult," I said. "I looked over, and McMillan was chanting with you. I thought to myself, Well, they've got him. Then I saw Jase and thought, Oh, no. They've got Jase too!"

Jase looked at me and said, "Let's play some cards, Si!"

Two years later, Phillip and I were driving to our friend SpongeBob's house for a poker game on my birthday. We stopped at my nephew Willie's restaurant in West Monroe to pick up food for the game.

"Hey, I'm staying in the truck," I said.

Phillip came out a few minutes later.

"There are four containers of food," he said. "You're going to have to come inside and help me carry them."

When I walked into Willie's Duck Diner, my family and most of my friends were there for a surprise birthday party in my honor. It's great to have so many loved ones and great friends who will go out of their way to make you feel special. Hey, they make me feel like my birthday is a national holiday every year.

*Everything that lives and moves about will be food for you.*

*Just as I gave you the green plants,*

*I now give you everything.*

—GENESIS 9:3 (NIV)

# CHAPTER 10

# SUICIDAL DEER

History books say that the largest typical white-tailed deer ever killed in the United States was shot by a hunter named James Jordan in Danbury, Wisconsin. In fact, it was the biggest white-tailed deer killed anywhere in the world for nearly eighty years.

Jordan was hunting with his friend Egus Davis on November 20, 1914, when they picked up the massive buck's tracks in the snow. Jordan shot the deer with his Winchester rifle and recovered it in the middle of the Yellow River. He dropped the buck off at the local taxidermist to be processed. When Jordan went back several months later to retrieve his mount and meat, he was stunned to learn that the taxidermist had moved to Florida!

Jordan believed his prized buck was gone forever. However, more than four decades later, Jordan's mount showed up at a yard sale in Sandstone, Minnesota. In 1971, the mount was shipped to Pennsylvania, where a panel of Boone and Crockett Club judges scored it. They declared it a new world record of 206⅛ points.

---

When Jordan went back to retrieve his
mount and meat, he was stunned to learn
the taxidermist had moved to Florida!

---

In 1978, two months after he died, Jordan was identified as the hunter who killed the record buck. His world record stood until 1993, when a hunter named Milo Hanson killed an even bigger whitetail buck in Saskatchewan, Canada.

Hey, I'm here to tell you that Jordan and Hanson are lucky their records are still standing. I actually missed the world's largest buck while hunting on my brother Phil's property about ten years ago. There's no doubt in my mind it would have been a world record. I saw the monster with my own eyes and it was definitely bigger, as God is my witness.

After spending most of the day in the woods, I spotted the buck right before the sun was starting to set. It was a cool autumn day, and I could see fog forming over the Ouachita River. There's something about being out in God's beautiful creation that fills me with si-renity and peace. I love that God made the world how He did and provided the food we need for the taking.

Well, when I saw that buck, it was like a scene out of the

movie *The Deer Hunter*. He stepped out of the fog and was probably two hundred yards from me. Hey, that buck was so big that I thought I might be dreaming.

My adrenaline started pumping and my hands were shaking. I was afraid to blink my eyes out of fear I'd spook the deer. I knew I couldn't miss the buck because I'd never see another one that big. I slowly and quietly eased my rifle to my shoulder and lined up the deer in my scope.

When I had the buck in the crosshairs, I gently pulled the trigger. I saw the bullet skip across the ground behind him. I fired five more shots at the deer, but missed every time. The buck took off running, and I never saw him again.

Unfortunately, the scope on my gun was a little bit off. Hey, I usually have it dialed in perfectly. I practice in my backyard by firing at a dime taped to the middle of a silver dollar. I shoot from twenty-five yards away and won't stop until it's precise.

After my last shot at the record buck, I made a good visualization in my mind of how big he really was. I knew it was bigger than any deer I'd ever seen, but smaller than an elephant or a rhinoceros. It was probably about four feet tall, but maybe more than six feet with its antlers.

When I got home, I pulled out a tape measure to figure out the width of the buck's rack. I pulled the tape out to one foot. *Nope, that ain't him,* I said to myself.

Then I pulled the measuring tape to two feet and then three feet. *Hey, that's a good deer, but it's not quite him,* I said.

Finally, after I pulled the tape out to four feet, I was satisfied. The buck I saw had a four-foot-wide rack, which would have undoubtedly set a world record. When I told Phil and his sons about seeing the buck, they told me I was telling another crazy story. In fact, Phil told me I must have seen an elk. There aren't any elk in Louisiana, Jack!

*Before I go hunting, I like to ask my nephews to walk right into me.*
*That way, I'll know my camouflage is working.*

Hey, I was so upset about missing that buck that I didn't sleep for three days. I knew I'd never see a deer that big again. Finding another one like him is one of the reasons I walk into the woods every morning during deer season.

Even though I would have been proud to mount that

head on my wall, the Robertson family has never been what I would consider trophy hunters. We don't hunt big game or big bucks for the sole purpose of hanging a deer head on the wall or putting a bear rug on the floor. We hunt for food and eat everything we shoot. I like deer hunting about as much as I like duck hunting, and you'll find me in a deer stand about every day during the season.

In the fall of 2015, I was invited to hunt deer at Lodge Creek Whitetails in Jacksboro, Texas. The Mitchell family, who owns the ranch, is committed to improving the size and quality of deer in Texas. They're good Christian people, who are committed to conservation and keeping the deer in Texas free of disease and overpopulation.

My buddy Phillip McMillan, his son Bryson, and my grandson Brady went to hunt at Lodge Creek Whitetails with me. Brady actually ended up shooting his first deer there, a nice eight-point buck. Bryson killed his first two deer too, and one of his ended up being the biggest buck out of our group.

When it was my turn to shoot, the Lodge Creek guides put me in a blind on top of a long food plot, which probably consisted of five or six acres. After about an hour, the guide told me, "Okay, Si, here comes the deer you want to shoot."

I looked down and saw an eight-point buck standing about 140 yards from me. Boom! I fired and missed. The deer took off running.

"What in the world?" I said. "How did I miss that deer?"

"Do you need to sight your rifle?" the guide asked me.

"You shot right over him. We didn't even see dirt kick up behind him."

"No, the rifle is fine," I said. "I shot a doe with it a few days ago."

Well, about twenty minutes later, the same deer walked back out onto the trail. I fired again—and missed. I ended up missing the deer seven times during the next two hours. I kept shooting and missing, and the deer kept coming back. I guess the deer knew I wasn't going to hit him! I was so mad that I grabbed my rifle and started to climb out of the deer stand.

The deer kept coming back.
I guess he knew I wasn't going to hit him!

"Hey, where you going?" the guide asked me. "Get back in here. There's still an hour of daylight left."

Just before dusk, the same deer walked out onto the path again. It must have been from Japan. It was a kamikaze deer if I'd ever seen one. This time, I set my rifle's crosshairs on the middle of his leg and under his belly. I gently pulled the trigger. I hit the deer square in his shoulder, which is exactly where I hadn't aimed. I shouldn't have killed the deer. As far as I'm concerned, he committed suicide.

When we returned home a few days later to West Monroe, Louisiana, I told my son, Scott, about what happened.

Only then did he inform me that he'd dropped my rifle out of a deer stand. The scope was out of whack. No wonder I shot and missed so many times.

Hey, I'll admit my vision isn't what it used to be. Shortly after the trip to Texas, I went deer hunting with my nephew Alan. We were walking to a couple of tree stands on Phil's property as the sun was rising.

"Man, did you see that?" Alan asked me.

"See what?" I said.

"A big falcon just flew over the top of us," he said.

"I didn't see it," I said.

A couple of minutes later, Alan said, "Man, did you see that?"

"See what?" I asked.

"A big black bear just walked behind those trees," he said.

"I didn't see it," I said.

After a few more minutes, Alan said, "Man, did you see that?"

I was starting to get a little agitated with him. I said, "Yeah, I saw it."

"Then why did you step in it?" Alan asked.

One thing I've learned over the years is that you have to be careful about where you step when you're hunting. You have to be aware of your environment and surroundings. If you're not paying attention, you might step on a snake, bear trap, fire ant hill, or wolverine.

After I was discharged from the army in 1971, Christine and I moved to Junction City, Arkansas, which is where Phil and his wife, Kay, were living. One day, Phil showed up at my house. He was excited and in a hurry.

"Hey, I found them," Phil said. "I know where there are hundreds of squirrels. Come on, there's only one hour of daylight left. It won't take us long to get enough for dinner."

Phil and I have been hunting squirrels our entire lives. When we were younger, squirrels were a regular part of our diet. Hey, when you can't afford to buy filet mignon and crab legs, you have to find another meat to eat. You need protein in your diet, and we ate squirrels, raccoons, possums, deer, fish, quail, and pheasant to supplement the fruits and vegetables that came from our family's garden.

Most people don't know that squirrels are actually very tasty. Squirrel meat is sweet because their diet consists mostly of berries and nuts. You can cook squirrels one hundred ways. I've eaten bacon-wrapped squirrel, fried squirrel, Crockpot squirrel, squirrel dumplings, squirrel with mushroom gravy, and squirrel stew. Hey, what's the best way to catch a squirrel? You climb up a tree and act like a nut, Jack!

Seriously, squirrels are fast animals and are difficult to kill. That's what makes hunting them so much fun. I grabbed my shotgun and a box of shells and jumped into Phil's truck. I wasn't going to pass up a chance to whack a few of those bushy-tailed varmints. Phil stopped his truck a few miles down the road from my house, and then we started walking into the woods. Phil was wearing only socks. He didn't wear shoes back then.

Phil and I decided to split up to cover more ground. Usually, we hunt squirrels together. One of us acts as a bush shaker; he's the guy who runs through the woods like a wild-man to get the squirrels on the move. The other one is the marksman; he's the guy who actually shoots the squirrels. Since we didn't have a lot of daylight left, we decided to split up to cover more ground.

Well, after about ten steps into the woods, I saw two cottonmouths and a copperhead. Hey, I don't like snakes, especially poisonous ones. Unfortunately, we have about every kind of venomous snake in Louisiana—cottonmouths, copperheads, coral snakes, and rattlesnakes. They can kill you with one bite!

When I saw the three snakes, I decided to leave them alone because I didn't want to waste my shotgun shells. But then I remembered I was going to have to exit the woods using the same path, and it was probably going to be dark when I left. So I turned around and fired. Boom! Boom! Boom!

My close encounter with the snakes had me a little on edge, so I walked down by the water and sat on a stump to catch my breath. After a couple of minutes, I heard a noise behind me. I looked and saw another cottonmouth. Boom! In about forty-five minutes in those woods, I shot and killed twenty-seven snakes! It must have sounded like the Battle of Saigon.

It was getting dark, and I had only three shells left. I knew I'd probably come across more snakes walking out of the woods, so I decided to call it a day. I hadn't killed a single squirrel. When I reached the edge of the woods, I saw the lights from Phil's truck.

"Boy, you must have worn 'em out!" Phil said. "I heard all those shots! How many did you kill?"

"I shot twenty-seven of them," I said.

"Were they young?" Phil asked.

"I don't know," I said.

"Well, where are they?" Phil asked.

"Right where I shot them," I said. "I didn't shoot squirrels, you idiot. I killed twenty-seven snakes! Hey, next time you want to come hunting out here, don't bother stopping by my house!"

―――――――――――

"I didn't shoot squirrels, you idiot," I told Phil.
"I killed twenty-seven snakes!"

―――――――――――

Hey, you wouldn't believe how easy it is for some hunters to get lost in the woods. The trees get pretty thick, and once you get turned around, it's very difficult to find your way out. Once the sun goes down, you're pretty much stuck there for the rest of the night. It's important to find landmarks and observe your surroundings. If you're not careful, you'll end up walking in circles for hours.

I'll never forget the time my nephews Jase and Willie went deer hunting with me and got lost in the woods. They were still pretty young, but they'd been hunting with me a few times. I thought they knew what they were doing.

When we arrived at our hunting camp that morning,

I told them I was going to walk to my tree stand. I told them to use the tree stands on the other side of the food plot. I instructed them to walk quietly around the perimeter of the field, so they wouldn't spook the deer.

"Hey, y'all stick together and don't get separated," I told them. "If you get lost, fire three shots in the air. I'll come find you."

Unfortunately, we didn't see many deer that day. I saw a couple of small does, but I was aiming for a big buck. I didn't hear the boys fire a single shot the entire day. When the sun started to set, I walked back to my truck and waited for Jase and Willie. Well, an hour went by and then another hour.

At about eight o'clock, I was starting to get pretty worried. I grabbed a flashlight and walked back into the woods. After searching for nearly an hour, I finally found them cuddled up together under a tree, cold and hungry.

"Hey, what happened to y'all?" I asked them. "I told y'all to fire three shots in the air, and I'd come find you."

"We fired *six* shots in the air," Willie said. "Then we ran out of arrows."

Now, I'm man enough to admit that Jase and Phil are probably the best hunters in our family. Obviously, Phil is the most skilled with a duck call and has mastered calling about every species: mallards, gadwalls, wood ducks, shovelers, pintails, wigeons, and teals.

Jase might be the best shooter, and he's definitely the most effective tracker. In fact, Jase is so adept at tracking a wounded animal that I'm convinced he could probably find a needle in a haystack. Jase is like a good bird dog. When he gets his nose on a scent, he's going to find what he's looking for. If we shoot a duck and don't kill it, we are legally required to make an attempt to find the wounded duck. Hey, I think it's the right thing to do. If I shoot a duck and it flies off, I don't want it suffering from its injuries. Tracking it down and putting it out of its misery is the humane thing to do.

When somebody wounds a duck, the first thing I'll hear is a big splash. Then I'll see Jase wading through the water with his shotgun.

> When somebody wounds a duck, I'll hear
> a big splash, then I'll see Jase wading
> through the water with his shotgun.

"Hey, where are you going?" I'll ask him.

"I'm going to find that mallard drake," Jase will say.

"I'll bet you five dollars you can't find it," I'll say.

Invaribly, Jase will be gone for about forty-five minutes, then he'll come back with the crippled duck—and a long, dramatic story about how he found it.

His stories usually go like this: "I knew the general area where the duck went down, but it probably covered a half acre. The wind was blowing pretty hard, but then I saw a small ripple on the water near a brush pile, kind of like when an acorn falls into the river. I saw a trail of bubbles, and then

I saw only the duck's eyes between four or five branches. He was hiding from me."

One time, Jase was gone for more than two hours while he tracked a crippled duck. We almost sent the National Guard to find him. When Jase finally returned, he was soaking wet and sweating profusely.

"Jase, you got us a story?" Phil asked him.

"Oh, do I have a story for you," Jase said.

"Jase, did you get wet?" Phil asked.

"Oh, did I get wet," Jase said.

Jase said he tracked the duck for more than two miles. By the time he reached it, he was so tired from running in his waders that he had to rest. He lay down on a mound we'd built with a bulldozer a few weeks earlier. As Jase closed his eyes, he heard a sound behind him. Then he saw an eight-point buck climb out of the water. The deer lay down on the same mound, looking the other way. The deer didn't even know Jase was behind him!

"Well, where's the deer?" I asked him.

"I didn't shoot it," he said. "I saw twenty-five or thirty mallards there. I didn't want to scare them away."

It wasn't the first time Jase failed to bag a deer while we were duck hunting. One day, he left the blind to go scouting for ducks to hunt the next day. He took a pirogue, which is a small boat, and went to an area on the other side of the lake. While Jase was scouting, he saw a twelve-point buck standing between two of our blinds. He thought to himself, *What idiot put that big fake buck out there in front of the duck blinds?*

All of the sudden, the big fake buck moved. Jase stood up in the pirogue and fired seven times and missed. He climbed out of the boat and fired again. When Jase arrived at where the deer was standing, he saw blood and tracked it for two hours. He never found the buck. He said it was one of the biggest deer he's ever seen.

And those boys say I like to tell a good story.

# HALLU-SI-NATIONS

## Black Panther

When I served in Vietnam in the late 1960s, the Vietcong were sometimes the least of our worries when we ventured into the jungle on missions. I'm telling you: there was danger wherever we went.

We had to worry about crocodiles and pythons in the water, and tigers, leopards, jackals, and marbled cats on dry land. Hey, that doesn't even include vampire bats that tried to suck your blood while you were sleeping. Those were some nasty suckers!

After I arrived in Can Tho in the Mekong Delta on October 19, 1968, some of my army buddies figured out I was really good at spotting snakes, tigers, and other deadly creatures from a mile away. I guess it's because I spent so much time in the woods as a kid.

Before too long, my army buddies started calling me Crazy Eyes because my vision was so good. They'd see me coming and say, "Here comes Crazy Eyes." Hey, the Good Lord blessed only a few of us with 30/30 vision. I might as well use it.

After I retired from the army and moved back to West Monroe, Louisiana, I spotted a black panther roaming my brother Phil's land a couple of times. It was a big, black cat that probably weighed about 125 pounds. It was about six feet long from its head to the tip of its tail.

Hey, my jaw dropped when I saw it because it is such a rare sight. It's like seeing Elvis at the shopping mall or my nephew

Willie doing something that requires exercise. In fact, I did a double take to make sure it was actually a panther. I know what I saw: it was definitely a black panther.

I saw the big black cat once when I was driving down a country road to Phil's house, and then again a couple of years later when I was driving an ATV to our duck blinds. Both times, the cat was about 350 yards away from me. It was too fast for me to catch, but I found its tracks. Boy, were they big! They were about the size of my hand.

Well, when I told Phil and his boys about what I saw, they told me I must have been seeing things. Jase told me it was probably a bobcat. Hey, news flash: bobcats don't have tracks that big, you idiot!

Phil and my nephews explained to me that black panthers don't exist in Louisiana. Hey, it is documented that there are black panthers in Arizona, Florida, and New Mexico, and there have been reported sightings in Texas. Billy "Red Dog" Phillips, who has hunted with us forever, even saw one in Arkansas.

Explain this: If there are black panthers in Arkansas, do they stop at the Louisiana border and turn around? Do they look at each other and say, "Nope, that's Louisiana. We're not allowed in there!"?

In one of the *Duck Dynasty* episodes during season three, Jase and Jep tried to prove that I've never seen a black panther. They had John Godwin, who works with us at Duck Commander, sneak about four hundred feet down a dirt road. Then he got down on all fours, crawled out of his hiding place, and roared like a black panther. He looked more like a black bear with a white beard to me.

Since that episode aired in March 2013, I've had hundreds of *Duck Dynasty* fans mail me letters and photos of black panthers in Louisiana. Hey, I'm not the only person who has seen them!

Well, I finally have obtained credible evidence that proves there are black panthers roaming in the Louisiana bayou, Jack! One of the guys who plays poker with me works for the electric company in West Monroe. During one of our games last year, Bull received an emergency service call to repair an electrical transformer that was knocked out during a bad thunderstorm.

When Bull arrived at the station to repair the transformer, he was shocked to find a dead black panther! The big cat had electrocuted itself, knocking out power in the process. It was stiff as a board. Hey, the cat probably weighed eighty or ninety pounds and had big white teeth like a vampire. It was a mean-looking cat, Jack!

Bull called me and told me about the dead panther.

"Hey, send that photo to Jase," I told him.

When Jase received the photograph of the panther, he said, "Nope. That's Photoshopped. There is no such thing as a black panther in Louisiana."

No matter what evidence I present, Jase will not believe that there are black panthers walking through the woods in Louisiana. He wouldn't believe they exist if one bit him on the butt! Hey, they are the very reason you don't walk to your deer stand at night! It's the reason I wait until sunrise to walk to mine.

Finally, after obtaining that photo evidence of their existence in Louisiana, I called a local game warden.

"If I see a black panther can I shoot it?" I asked him.

"No," he said. "Black panthers don't exist in Louisiana."

No matter what evidence I present, Jase will
not believe that there are black panthers
walking through the woods in Louisiana.

Well, consider it open season on black panthers in Louisiana. I can't be punished for shooting something that doesn't exist.

*Yes, my soul, find rest in God;*

*my hope comes from him.*

—PSALM 62:5 (NIV)

# CHAPTER 11

# HOMES OF HOPE

Hey, as far as I'm concerned, the two greatest sounds in the world are a child's laughter and the splash of a mallard duck crashing into the water on a cool, crisp morning on the Louisiana bayou. It doesn't get any better than that, Jack!

The absolute best part of my life is meeting a child and making him or her laugh uncontrollably. Thankfully, the Good Lord has blessed me with the ability to make people laugh and smile, especially kids. First comes their giggle. Then comes their belly laugh, when they start grabbing their stomachs and fall on the ground. Then comes their screams that they're going to pee their pants. Hey, it works every time. It's like magic.

When I meet a kid at one of my public appearances or at the grocery store, I tell him or her to look deep into my eyes.

"What do you see?" I'll ask them.

"I see a bearded old dude," he or she will say.

*There is nothing that brings more joy to my heart than being with children.
That's why I've become so involved in several children's charities.*

"Hey, look deeper," I'll say. "You're not looking deep enough into my eyes. Look again and tell me what you see."

"I still see an old dude with a beard," they'll say.

"No, there's a ten-year-old kid in there trying to get out," I say. "He's trapped inside a sixty-seven-year-old body!"

I can't pass up an opportunity to make a child laugh and smile. Anything that has something to do with kids, hey, I'm all in. In 2013, I was asked to play the voice of Silas the Wise Old Okra on the *Veggie Tales* DVD called *Merry Larry and the*

*True Light of Christmas*. I'll admit that I was a little green at playing a vegetable, but it was a lot of fun. Hey, I ate so much stewed okra and tomatoes when I was a kid that I still slide out of bed every night.

The next year, I co-authored a children's book titled *Uncle Si the Christmas Elf*. The idea actually came from Ashley Howard Nelson, who is Korie Robertson's sister—and Ashley did most (that means *all*) of the writing. In the story, Santa asks Uncle Si for help and commissions him as an elf to make a special toy for a little boy who wouldn't have a Christmas if Si didn't help. You wouldn't believe the get-up I had to wear!

Hey, I miss being a kid. I miss learning to ride a bike for the first time. I miss sliding down the stairs on pillows. I miss catching frogs, lizards, and fireflies (but definitely not snakes). I miss riding a roller coaster eight times at the country fair, and then asking my dad to "do it again." I miss Trapper Keepers, pizza Fridays in the lunchroom, Saturday-morning cartoons, hide-and-seek, recess with my friends, and never having to sign a check or pay a bill.

When we're kids, we can't wait to grow up. When we're grown up, we miss being a kid. As adults, we get so caught up in the hustle and bustle of everyday life that we don't have time to stop and giggle, tell a knock-knock joke, scream about someone sitting on a whoopee cushion, or laugh so hard that milk shoots out of our noses. Hey, there have been plenty of times when I wanted to go back to being nine years old, when my only worries were about whether or not my brothers put my hand in warm water while I was sleeping. There's no doubt about it: if I had a time machine, I'd go back to my childhood.

Hey, my wife, Christine, would probably say that I never grew up. I still nap whenever I want. I drink iced tea whenever I want. A skateboard and pogo stick are my preferred methods of transportation. I wear Mickey Mouse pajamas and eat Fruity Pebbles for lunch. I watch *SpongeBob Square-Pants* and *Scooby-Doo*. Hey, I'd much rather eat chicken fingers and French fries than filet mignon and asparagus for dinner—in fact, it's what I eat six nights a week (Chick-fil-A is closed on Sundays, if you didn't know).

---

I wear Mickey Mouse pajamas and
eat Fruity Pebbles for lunch.

---

Even after sixty-eight years, I'm still a kid at heart. I think that's one of the reasons I have become so involved in children's ministries and charities. There's nothing that breaks my heart more than hearing about a neglected or abused child. I can't imagine what would make an adult be so mean to a child, especially a parent who abuses or neglects his or her own kids.

According to the National Children's Alliance, more than fifteen hundred children died from abuse and neglect in the United States in 2013. In that same year, children's advocacy centers across the country served nearly 700,000 child victims of abuse and neglect. About 80 percent of the victims were abused or neglected by one or more of their parents. Child abuse sickens me, and it has to stop. Children are our greatest gift, and we have to make sure that every child is being loved and properly cared for.

I have been blessed by the Good Lord to be in a position to help charities and ministries financially. I like to focus on local charities that help people in West Monroe, Louisiana, and other parts of my home state, but there are exceptions. One of my favorite ministries is the Louisiana Methodist Children's Home, in Ruston, Louisiana, where my good friend Phillip McMillan works. It serves thousands of abused and neglected children around the state, and I've made multiple appearances at fund-raisers and other events to help it raise money for its homes.

Another charity I have become intimately involved with is Homes of Hope for Children in Purvis, Mississippi. Its executive director and founder, Dr. Michael Garrett, is a survivor of child abuse. When Michael was young, he was abused both physically and emotionally.

When Michael's mother became seriously ill and was unable to care for her three children, Michael and his two sisters were forced to live in foster homes; Michael was in the third grade. Family services separated Michael from his two sisters. His sisters were placed in a home with loving, caring foster parents. Unfortunately, Michael was not.

Often, older boys in the home beat him and shot him

with a BB gun. Also, because Michael was overweight, he was constantly referred to as Tugboat. Michael's foster parents kept him from visiting his sisters.

After spending a year in foster care, Michael's mother was well enough to regain custody of her children. The day he left the foster home was one of the best days of his life. Unfortunately, their reunion didn't last long. His mother was physically, emotionally, and financially unable to care for her kids, so Michael and his sisters were placed at the Louisiana Baptist Children's Home in Monroe. While Michael longed to be with his mother, he was happy that he was at least living with his sisters again.

Because of Michael's past experiences in foster care, he was anxious about living in the children's home. It was another new and unfamiliar environment. His first days at the children's home were spent fighting back tears and worrying about his future. However, Michael soon realized that his new home was different. He lived on the same campus with his sisters, and they attended the same school and church. They were allowed to be a part of each other's lives. Michael and his sisters were a family again.

Soon after Michael and his sisters moved into the children's home, he realized they were surrounded by Jesus Christ's unconditional love through the people that served in the ministry. They were living in a good, Christian environment with adults who genuinely loved and cared for them. Michael felt safe for the first time in his life. More than anything else, he was allowed to be a kid again.

Michael lived at the Louisiana Baptist Children's Home for seven years. While living there, God began teaching him vital aspects of the ministry. His guidance helped Michael realize, create, and develop his own vision for a children's home for abused and neglected children—even as that very ministry was meeting his own needs. Before Michael graduated from high school he left the children's home to live with Travis and Virginia Eaton, whose family he had grown very close to. With the continued support of the children's home and his new family, Michael found himself in a truly blessed situation.

Shortly after Michael graduated from high school, he surrendered himself full-time to the ministry. He wanted to dedicate the rest of his life to ensuring that other children in situations similar to his own received the same life-changing opportunities he was given. Living at the children's home afforded Michael a chance to escape the destructive cycle of abuse and poverty that is unnecessarily endured by so many children. After the Louisiana Baptist Children's Home saved his life, Michael wanted to make a difference in other children's lives as well.

In 2006, Michael, his wife, Julie, and their infant son, Caleb, moved to Hattiesburg, Mississippi. He started to put his vision for a children's home into action. It wasn't easy. Every time Michael hit a roadblock, he put his faith in God to make his dream come to life so he could help neglected boys and girls. God rescued him from the brink of failure many times. Michael spoke to churches and civic organizations across the South to raise money for his children's home, and he applied for grants from foundations, charitable organizations, and corporations.

In July 2010, Homes of Hope for Children completed construction of a boys' cottage on forty-two acres in Purvis, Mississippi. A girls' cottage was built and opened the next year. Currently, Michael and his ministry provide a home for fifteen boys and girls who come from abusive and broken homes. In 2016, another home will open on their campus, bringing the total number of children being served to twenty-one. His long-term goal is to have six cottages to care for more than forty-two children.

After coming from dysfunctional homes, the children live in a stable, loving environment with other kids. Married couples live with the children in the homes. A licensed counselor works with the children to help them heal mentally and spiritually.

The kids who live at Homes of Hope for Children attend the same schools and church, and even take summer vacations together. The homes offer them long-term stability. The kids can live in the cottages until they turn eighteen. Once they graduate from high school, Michael places them in on-campus apartments, as long as they're attending college or learning a vocation.

One of my favorite things about Homes of Hope for Children is the fact that they fight legal battles to get children out of a dangerous home or to keep them from going back into one. Michael's ministry is a faith-based children's home that partners with grandparents and other family members and goes to court to protect innocent children. This ministry is proving that a faith-based ministry can do everything for children that we currently trust the government to do. But this ministry does it better.

I can't say enough about Michael and what he's doing. I've fallen in love with his ministry and how far he'll go to keep his kids safe. He had a very bad experience in foster homes as a kid, and he has taken a vow that he isn't going to let that happen to the children under his care. He knows what it feels like to be neglected and abused. His children are going to be loved unconditionally, and their physical, spiritual, and emotional needs are going to be met. Hey, if that ain't love, I don't know what is, Jack!

I've attended fund-raisers for Michael's charity and visited the homes on several occasions. I've met the children under his care, like Javier, Daniel, Julianna, Gavriel, and little Cameron, and they're loving, happy kids. As you can see from the picture on page 170, Cameron and I are good buddies. The children under Michael's care are a lot better off than many because they're living in nurturing homes. The fact that so many of them are able to live with their siblings makes a world of difference in their lives. Children should never be separated from their brothers and sisters.

Hey, I only wish there was enough time in the day to help every ministry and charity that reaches out to us for help. We've been involved with dozens of great organizations, including Samaritan's Purse, Christian Relief Fund, St. Jude Children's Research Hospital, and the Wiregrass Children's Home in Dothan, Alabama.

During the past few years, I've been amazed at how resilient children are and how much they're willing to help each other. I wish adults acted more like kids sometimes, that's for sure. The world would be a better place if we all slowed down, smiled, and laughed uncontrollably like a kid.

---

The world would be a better place if we all slowed
down, smiled, and laughed uncontrollably.

---

I'll never forget meeting a ten-year-old boy named Mitchell Underwood in August 2013 during one of our appearances in Mountain Grove, Missouri. The young boy waited in line and brought me a bag of duck decoys to autograph. He told me that the decoys were going to be auctioned off to help pediatric cancer patients at St. Jude. I couldn't believe a boy that young could be so selfless. I told him his good deed wouldn't go unnoticed by the man upstairs.

I'm trying to be more like Mitchell. I think one of the reasons I try to be benevolent is because so many people helped my family when I was young. I grew up in a small log cabin in Vivian, Louisiana. The cabin was really rustic; we used an outhouse and didn't even have hot water to take a bath. My parents, Merritt and James Robertson, had five boys, and I was the youngest. Jimmy Frank was my oldest brother, followed by Harold, Tommy, and Phil. I had an older sister, Judy, and then my younger sister, Jan, came along a few years after I was born.

There were nine people living in the log cabin, and most of our food came from the fruit and vegetable garden my parents planted every spring. My brothers and I hunted deer, birds, squirrels, and just about anything else we could eat. Our eggs came from the chickens on our farm, and the milk and cheese came from our cows. My parents didn't have a lot of money, and there usually wasn't much left over to buy groceries after they'd paid the bills. We only had enough money to buy the bare necessities, like flour, sugar, and coffee.

My family had some very difficult times when I was young, especially after we moved to Dixie, Louisiana. My mother was plagued by mental illness and spent a lot of time at the state psychiatric hospital. During one of the times she was hospitalized, my father was badly injured while working on an oil rig. He fell and broke his back and was forced to wear a plaster cast for more than a year. He couldn't work, and his disability checks weren't enough to pay our bills and feed us.

I'll never forget how the people in our small community rallied around my family. They weren't much better off than us financially, but they found a desire in their hearts to help a desperate neighbor. I'll never forget finding baskets of eggs, bread, and canned goods on our back steps. We didn't know who dropped it off, but the food meant we wouldn't go hungry. On Christmas morning, the African American lady who lived down the road from us left a basket of oranges, candy, and other goodies for my siblings and me. She wanted to make sure we didn't miss out on Christmas.

Listen here, friend, it is our Christian duty to help others in need. In the Bible, the word *charity* almost always means love. In Jesus' parable of the sheep and goats, He says, *"Then the King will say to those on his right, 'Come, you who are blessed by my Father; take your inheritance, the kingdom prepared for you since the creation of the world. For I was hungry and you gave me something to eat, I was thirsty and you gave me something to drink, I was a stranger and you invited me in, I needed clothes and you clothed me, I was sick and you looked after me, I was in prison and you came to visit me'"* (Matthew 25:34–36). Indeed, when we care for someone in need, we do the will of Christ.

Hey, help others as much as you can. Take care of the sick and needy in your community and contribute to charitable organizations like Habitat for Humanity, Goodwill, and the Salvation Army. Hey, don't give away money you can't afford to live without. If all you can donate is a few dollars every month, then only give away a few dollars. I'm sure if you take a hard look at what you're spending your money on, you can find a few extra dollars for charity in your budget. If nothing else, put a shoe box on the counter and throw your loose change into it every day. I think you'd be surprised at how much is in there at the end of every month. Give it to your church or a charity to help those people in need.

If you aren't able to give money, then donate your time and talents to battered women's shelters, food banks, and churches. Volunteer to read to at-risk children or mentor kids at the Boys & Girls Clubs or the YMCA. You will be surprised at how much impact you can have on a young person's life. Every kid needs a good role model. Lord knows there aren't enough men being real fathers in the world today. Spend an hour or two every week mentoring a boy or girl who doesn't have a good role model at home.

Now, you might be thinking, "How is giving my money away going to help me?" First of all, you shouldn't be thinking that way. You're doing it because it's our Christian duty and it's the right thing to do. But you might be surprised to learn that it can help you in more ways than you can imagine. There's a lot to be said for helping a struggling family build a home, or helping a sick child go on a vacation to the beach or Disney World. It's the most rewarding feeling in the world, and it might even inspire others to help as well. If we start caring for each other again, like our neighbors helped my family and me so many years ago, the world will be a much better place. For whatever reason, we've gotten away from loving and caring for each other.

Being charitable and helping others will give you a peaceful and restful heart, and there's not a better feeling in the world than that, folks. Hey, if nothing else, it will make you realize how lucky and fortunate you are to have your good health, a roof over your head, food on your table, and clothes on your back. So often we take those things for granted, and don't appreciate them. When we decide to help others in need, it makes us take a good look at our own lives. Only then will we realize how much the Almighty has blessed us. I know the Robertson family has been truly blessed, and I'm so thankful we're in a position to help others.

# HALLU-SI-NATIONS
## Stickball

As I mentioned earlier, I've always been very interested in Native American culture. I think my interest probably started when I was a kid. My uncle Mack Hobbs had a massive collection of more than five thousand arrowheads, tomahawks, and other artifacts.

Mack found many of his artifacts on my brother Phil's property near the Ouachita River in West Monroe, Louisiana. One year, Mack shot a deer and found half of an eight-inch spearhead while he was tracking it. The next year, he shot another deer in the same area and found the other half. What are the odds? His collection is now on display at Louisiana State University.

During the past few years, I've had several opportunities to visit with Native American tribes around the country. I spent time with the Seminoles in Florida and the Cherokees in North Carolina. I'm actually one-sixteenth Cherokee Indian; my great-great grandmother was a full-blooded Cherokee.

I've also visited the Choctaw in Mississippi. The Choctaw have been in the southeastern United States since the sixteenth century. They fought bloody battles against Spanish explorer Hernando de Soto's armies in 1540, and they fought against the British in the French and Indian Wars in the mid-eighteenth century.

After the Civil War, our government seized millions of

acres of the Choctaw's ancestral lands. The Choctaw were the first tribe to walk the Trail of Tears to reservations west of the Mississippi River, and nearly 2,500 of them died along the way. Willie's wife, Korie, actually has two Choctaw chiefs in her lineage.

The Choctaw Indians who are in Mississippi today are a proud and generous people. When I visited with them, they were holding their annual World Series Stickball. The people who organized the event where I appeared told me it was like going to the Super Bowl.

"We used to play stickball as kids," I said. "I know everything there is to know about stickball."

*Hey, if you think football is a physical sport, you should see the Choctaw tribe play stickball. It's a man's sport, Jack!*

Hey, we couldn't afford baseballs, bats, and gloves when I was a kid, so we used a broomstick and a ball of socks. I'll never forget when my older sister, Judy, made her first batch of cat head biscuits from scratch. They were green and hard. They tasted awful, but they made pretty good baseballs. We played with them until they busted. Judy later became a very good cook, but her first endeavor wasn't very promising.

When I arrived at World Series Stickball in Philadelphia, Mississippi, I couldn't believe the scene. There were hundreds of people on both sides. There was a loud cadence of drumbeats from the stands as the game was being played. I noticed about ten ambulances waiting in an end zone of the football field where they were playing. I thought to myself, *What in the world is this all about?*

Hey, stickball is a contact sport, to say the least. It's a combination of rugby, football, hockey, and basketball. It's a lot like lacrosse, but it's much more violent. Dozens of men carry two long sticks called *kaboccas* to catch and pass a buckskin ball called a *towa*. You can't touch the towa with your hands. The objective of the game is to knock or throw the towa at a twelve-foot-tall wooden pole on the opponent's side of the field.

Getting to the pole is where it gets dangerous. Players tackle each other and throw opponents to the ground. Their collisions are as violent as in football, but they don't wear pads or helmets. The only time action stops is when an injured player can't get off the field. Hey, it's a man's sport, Jack!

---

Their collisions are as violent as in football,
but they don't wear pads or helmets.

---

The Choctaw take stickball very seriously. Their ancestors played the sport hundreds of years ago, and it's an important part of their heritage. Back then the Choctaw used the game to settle disputes. The poles might have been separated by one mile. Tribe members from ages ten to seventy played in the games. The games would last for days. Instead of going to war, they played stickball. Hey, wouldn't it be a better world if that's how we settled our differences today?

I led the Beaver Dam team onto the field for the last game of the night. Beaver Dam is one of the sport's best teams, and I was wearing one of their red jerseys. I was also wearing a colorful Mohawk headdress that lit up. Hey, when I was a kid, every summer when school ended, one of the first things my brothers and I did was cut our hair into Mohawks. I guess that's why my momma told her friends, "I've got a bunch of Indians running around my house."

At halftime, I walked to the other side of the field. The opposing team's fans started booing me and throwing tomatoes and cucumbers at me! I quickly returned to the Beaver Dam side.

Hey, maybe the Choctaw aren't as gentle as I believed!

*"Come, follow me and I will make you fishers of men."*

—MATTHEW 4:19 (NIV)

# CHAPTER 12

# FISHING FOR MEN

Fishing is about the most relaxing thing to do in the world. There's nothing more peaceful than sitting in a boat on a hot summer day and throwing a line into the water. It's only you and the sounds of nature. That guy from *Parks and Recreation* is right: fishing is a lot like yoga, except you still get to kill something.

I've been fishing my entire life. From the time I was a little boy, I caught fish in ponds, lakes, rivers, creeks, swamps, reservoirs, and mud puddles. I've caught catfish, goldfish, bass, crappie, trout, gar, carp, and buffalo. That's what I love most about fishing. There's always somewhere new to go, and you never know what's going to be on the end of your hook when you reel it in.

Well, fishing is that way for most folks. I've spent so much of my life on the water that I have developed the uncanny sense of knowing what species of fish is on my hook before I even reel it in. It's like having a sixth sense, Jack! A lot of people would like to have it, but only a few of us have been blessed with that God-given ability.

When I was stationed at Fort Polk in Leesville, Louisiana, in the late 1970s, I had a couple of buddies in the Fifth Aviation Battalion who were big fishermen. They liked to go camping and fishing during R&R, and they often pestered me about going with them. But I had two young kids at home, and I knew I had better odds of being elected to Congress than spending an entire weekend on the lake with my friends.

Luckily for me, Christine took our children to Kentucky for a week to see her parents. As soon as they were gone, I loaded up my truck and went camping with my buddies. We headed to the Toledo Bend Reservoir, which sits between Louisiana and Texas. It is the fifth-largest man-made body of water in the US, covering more than 180,000 acres. Toledo Bend Reservoir is full of striped bass, largemouth bass, bluegill, flathead catfish, blue catfish, and a lot of other species of fish. It's one of the best fishing holes in the world.

After we set up camp along one of the back channels, I showed my buddies how to set up a throw line. I'd been doing it for years. Growing up, I spent nearly every weekend and most summer days with my older brothers fishing for catfish on the Ouachita River. We'd put twelve hooks on a throw line and tie it off to a willow branch and brick. We'd bait the hooks with live brim, and then one of us would throw the brick into the water. We'd run four or five throw lines at a time and have as many as sixty hooks in the water at once.

*Until recently, I'd only fished in lakes, rivers, ponds,
and mud puddles. I've learned the ocean is like a box of
chocolates—you never know what you're going to get!*

Since I wasn't very familiar with Toledo Bend Reservoir,
I decided to use only one throw line. I wanted to make sure
we got a bite before I threw five or six of them in the water.
Once the throw line was set, we built a campfire and caught a
couple of fish with rods and reels to fry for dinner. Then we

sat back and waited for the throw line to get full. As the sun started to set, I heard the first splash.

"Hey, that's a flathead," I said.

A few minutes later, there was another splash.

"Oh, that sounds like a channel catfish," I said.

Then there was another flathead, two more channel cats, and then another flathead.

"Robertson, you're nuts," one of my buddies said. "There's no way in the world you know what kind of fish they are by the sounds of the splashes."

———

"There's no way in the world you know what kind of fish they are by the sounds of the splashes."

———

"Hey, just wait and see," I said. "I'm telling you that I know exactly what is on those hooks!"

A while later, I heard a bigger splash.

"Hmmm," I said. "I'm not exactly sure what that is."

Once I was confident the throw line was full of fish, it was time to pull it in. Hey, our final catch: three flatheads, three channel cats, and one snapping turtle. Just call me Nostradamus, Jack.

In addition to knowing what fish sound like on a throw line, I'm also pretty adept at knowing exactly where fish are swimming. Hey, I have a nose for fish, Jack! It's really important when you're jugging for catfish. If you've never been jugging, it's a great way to catch a lot of fish. It doesn't cost much and doesn't take a lot of time, either.

The only things you need for jugging are jugs, fishing line, hooks, sinkers, and bait. You can use about any kind of jug with a handle: milk jugs, peanut oil jugs, or water jugs. Tie a five-foot line to each of the handles, and then tie them together. That will keep them from floating away. Then tie a hook and sinker to each jug. Make sure the weights are heavy enough to keep the jugs in place. Now it's time for the bait. Hey, catfish will eat about anything that smells: shad, chicken livers, crawfish, hot dogs, goat scrotum, and frogs.

Once the jugs are set, you can sit in your boat or wait on shore until the catfish are biting. When the jugs start bouncing, flipping, and shaking, it's time to pick them up and see what's on the hook. We've caught monster catfish this way. We mostly go jugging in the Ouachita River, but I've done it in ponds and lakes too.

I'll never forget the time I was jugging at a pond not far from our house. I'd already set the jugs out that morning. When I returned with a bucket of chicken livers to bait the hooks, I heard a lot of giggling as I walked to the pond. I thought somebody was trying to steal my jugs! But then I saw a pile of clothes on the boat dock. Four women were skinny-dipping in the pond!

"Hey, y'all shouldn't be in there," I said.

"Well, we're not going to get out with you standing there," one of the ladies said.

"That's fine," I said. "I'm only here to feed the alligators."

Ice fishing is another great way to fish, but I've only done it once. It doesn't get cold enough in northern Louisiana to freeze over lakes and rivers. But during one particularly cold winter, I found a small pond where I could try it. I set up my tent, packed a lunch, and grabbed my ice pick and rod and reel. When I started picking at the ice, I heard a very loud voice say, "There are no fish under the ice!"

I looked around and didn't see anyone. Was it the Almighty talking to me?

After a few minutes, I started picking at the ice again. Then I heard the same voice: "There are no fish under the ice!"

"God, is that you?" I said, as I looked up at the sky.

"No, you idiot, it's the manager," the voice answered. "This is an ice skating rink, not a fishing pond."

After spending twenty-four years in the army, I was forced to retire on January 31, 1993. Christine and I moved from Germany to Hollytree, Alabama, which is located at the foot of the Appalachian Mountains, not far from the Tennessee border. I thought fishing and hunting would keep me busy, but it just wasn't enough. I was bored, so I took a job as a groundskeeper at a golf course near our house.

There was a pond next to every green on the golf course. That meant there were eighteen fishing holes for me. Unfortunately, it took a while for me to persuade the superintendent to let me fish in them. He finally agreed, though, and I loved fishing in those ponds.

There were enormous crappie and bass in those ponds. In hindsight, they might have been supersized because fertilizer from the greens was running off into the ponds. And they might have been toxic, but they sure tasted fine. Hey, they're a lot of fun to catch when they're that big!

One day, I was fishing in the pond next to the eleventh hole, and another foreman from Georgia drove up on his lawnmower. I cast a line to the middle of the pond. Immediately, I felt a big bite.

"Man, that's a five- or six-pound bass," the foreman said. "You better reel that sucker in."

I pulled on my rod and hooked the fish. It was a four-pound crappie, which was one of the biggest I'd ever seen. I'm telling you: the fish was perfect. There wasn't a fin or scale out of place. It was a beautiful fish, and I knew it was going to taste great with butter, cornmeal, and salt and pepper.

I grabbed a stringing line out of my tackle box and ran it through the fish's mouth.

"Man, don't put that on a stringer," the foreman said. "That's the biggest crappie I've ever seen. You need to put that fish in your truck on ice. You need to get it mounted."

"Hey, my truck is one thousand yards up the hill," I said. "It will take me too long to get up there and back. The fish are biting, and I am not leaving this pond."

I threw the crappie back into the pond, and tied the stringer to a small tree on the bank. I ended up catching about eight or nine more crappie, along with a couple of nice-size bass. At the end of the day, I pulled the stringer out of the water. Much to my horror, a snapping turtle had eaten every fish on the line. The only thing left was the prized crappie's head! My wife still hates seeing the fish's head mounted over our front door.

---

Much to my horror, a snapping turtle
had eaten every fish on the line.

---

The next day, I fished in the pond next to the eighteenth hole and caught twenty-five crappie and about a half dozen bass. I'd learned my lesson. Instead of tying the fish to a stringer, I threw them into the back of a golf cart where I had some ice. As I was driving back to the maintenance shop, the superintendent stopped me.

"Hey, bring me back a couple of bottles of water," he said. "It's getting hot out here."

Then he looked in the back of my golf cart.

"Good grief," he said. "Where did you get all of those fish?"

"Out of that pond!" I said. "Now you know why I pestered you about fishing in them."

Catching crappie and brim is usually pretty relaxing. It doesn't require a lot of work, and it's not nearly as dangerous as fishing on the river or in the ocean. About the only risk is falling off the dock and into the water. Or at least that's what I thought.

One summer day, I spent several hours fishing for crappie from the boat dock at Phil's house. I caught a crappie that weighed about a pound and a half. It was big enough to keep and eat, so I turned to put the fish in my cooler. Well, I turned the wrong way and immediately felt a piercing pain in my side. Even after I wrapped my chest in tight bandages, the pain didn't go away for three days.

Finally, Christine made me go to the doctor. He took an X-ray of my chest and saw two broken ribs. The doctor gave me a shot for the pain, and I recovered after a few more weeks. Hey, I never knew a fish so small could have such a big bite!

One kind of fishing I'd never experienced until recently was deep-sea fishing. Hey, my number-one rule in life for a long time was that I'd never get into a boat and go so far out in the water that I couldn't see the shore. I wanted to be close enough to swim back to land if something happened. When you fish with the guys I fish with, there's plenty that can go wrong.

I'd heard horror stories about deep-sea fishing: seasickness, falling overboard, boats breaking down, hurricanes, twelve-foot swells, sharks, jellyfish, and stingrays. I didn't want any part of it. I'd much rather fish in fresh water, where my only worries are about my nephew Willie hooking me in the ear or catching the Loch Ness Monster.

Well, a couple of years ago, I was invited to go deep-sea fishing in Key West, Florida. I agreed to go after I checked the captain's credentials and thoroughly inspected his boat. Then I did some research on how to prevent motion sickness. The last thing I wanted was to get seasick fifty miles from shore. I didn't want to be hanging over the boat for eight hours, chumming up the ocean with unsweetened tea. When I boarded the boat that morning, I had $B_{12}$ patches behind both ears and relief bands on both of my wrists. I was also sucking on a lemon.

When the captain saw me, he said: "Hey, are we going fishing or are you going into space?"

I ended up having a fantastic time fishing with Captain Max Hardin and his crew. Their eighty-foot boat, *The Easy Rider,* is aptly named. It's like fishing from a floating house. The best part: there are bedrooms below deck. I was able to nap until the crew woke me up when fish were biting. Hey, we even went skeet shooting from the back of the boat! Max and his sons sure know how to keep a country boy happy.

We went out into the Gulf of Mexico and caught red snapper, Goliath grouper, lemon sharks, and yellowtail snapper. I also caught a twenty-five-pound barracuda. I'd never seen so many teeth on a fish! About two hours into our trip, my buddy Phillip McMillan woke me up.

"Si, you have to come see these flying fish."

"Hey, there's no such thing as flying fish," I said. "Fish don't have wings."

"Hey, you have to come see them to believe it," he said.

I climbed up to the crow's nest and couldn't believe what I saw. There were fish flying out of the water and staying airborne from about five hundred to one thousand feet. They were like cruise missiles! Hey, I started looking for my shotgun!

On our last stop of the trip, we caught yellowfin and blackfin tuna at the base of an oil rig that was about fifty miles offshore. Hey, reeling in a 120-pound tuna in the ocean is like trying to pull a John Deere tractor with a bungee cord.

The fish is basically swimming at thirty miles per hour trying to save its life, while you're fighting to hang on and reel it in.

After forty-five minutes of fighting the fish—and making sure it didn't pull me into the ocean—a crewman finally gaffed the tuna and pulled it into the boat. Hey, Mike Tyson's bouts didn't last that long. It took all of my strength to hold the tuna up for photographs.

After Max and his boys moved their boat to Freeport, Texas, I went fishing with them a couple of other times. We caught pompano, mahimahi, triggerfish, and a big mess of trout. During our last trip with Max, a crewmember who was battling terminal cancer went with us. We prayed with him and lifted him up to the Almighty. At the end of the day, Max made me an honorary member of the Harbor Master Club. I'm proud to say I'm a card-carrying member.

Along with duck hunting, fishing is one of my favorite things to do. Jesus told us that He would make us "fishers of men." Jesus saw Simon and Peter casting their nets and said to them, *"Come, follow me and I will make you fishers of men"* (Matthew 4:19). His instructions were simple: Follow me, and I will take care of the rest.

Jesus told us that He would make us "fishers of men."

As Christians, we have to remember that fish don't come to us. We have to go find them, cast a line, hook them, and reel them in. We're not going to catch many fish for Jesus from our church pews. We have to go into our neighbor-hoods and communities to spread His Word. It's our duty as Christians. We only have to cast the line—Jesus will do the catching.

Like when I'm fishing for crappie or yellowfin tuna, shar-ing my faith requires plenty of patience. I can't tell you how many times I've spent several hours in a boat and come home empty-handed. Hey, some days the fish are biting and some days they aren't.

Sure, luck might be involved in fishing, but you also have to possess good instincts and skills. The same is true with spreading the Good News. I know I'm not going to land every nonbeliever, but I'm going to keep casting my line in case I do. There are plenty of big ones still out there, and it's our job to find them. Jesus expects it from us.

# HALLU-SI-NATIONS
## Bowfishing

Hey, do you know what you get when you combine fishing with archery? Yeah, a bunch of fish with holes in them! I'd never been bowfishing until the opening day of duck season in 2015. I'm not sure I've ever had more fun.

We were hunting on the bayou of Plaquemines Parish, which is a little south of New Orleans. Josh Galt, who owns Scale Damage Bowfishing, took us fishing that night with a compound bow that's rigged with a special rod and reel.

As the sun was setting, we took an airboat into the marsh, and one of Josh's deckhands turned on a big spotlight. I saw fish everywhere in the water. I shot fish with arrows and then reeled them in. We caught redfish, speckled trout, garfish, drum, and flounder. It's one of the biggest adrenaline rushes I've ever experienced.

I believe that God brings people into our lives to fulfill His purpose for us. He also brings people into our lives to teach us things or to remind of us something we might have forgotten.

---

I believe that God brings people into our lives to fulfill His purpose for us.

---

I think Josh Galt is one of the people God placed in my life. Josh grew up in Louisiana. His mother was a faithful Christian, and her father was a preacher. But their life was far from joyful.

Josh had a tough time growing up. His parents divorced when he was four years old, and he moved into low-income housing with his mother and older brother. After they went bowling one night, they returned to their apartment and everything was gone—even the Christmas tree.

Because of his resentment about his father's leaving, Josh had trouble with authority. He had a short temper and often turned to fighting to solve his problems. He was kicked out of high school as a junior, and it seemed that he was headed down a tragic road.

Finally, Josh decided it was time to turn his life around. He completed his GED and enrolled at a community college to study nursing.

Josh started running airboats and guiding fishing expeditions when he was seventeen years old. He loved being on the water, and it made him realize that there was more to life than partying and being a knucklehead. Josh started his own bowfishing company and is still running it today. Now he even has his own TV show, *Southern Chaos*, which is broadcast on the Sportsman Channel.

When Josh was twenty-four years old, he married his long-time girlfriend, Ashton.

On December 17, 2012, Josh was on his way to brush his duck blinds when he received a telephone call from his grandfather. His mother had died. She was forty-five years old.

After his mother's death, Josh turned to what she had always relied on—faith in Jesus Christ. Josh had peace knowing that his mother was no longer in pain and that God had welcomed her to heaven with open arms. Josh knew it's where she needed to be.

Josh's life and faith remind me of God's purpose for each of our lives and the way God can redeem anyone who's willing and bring about His good.

Jesus gave us a gift that no one can take away—His blood. It's up to us to accept His precious gift of salvation. No matter the problems we might be dealing with or the trouble we're facing, we have to understand that nothing is too great for the Lord to control. God is bigger than any problem we'll face, as long as we put our trust and faith in Him.